ENNEAGRAM

The Complete Guide to Personality Types and Self-discovery Unleash the Empath in You

(Effective Steps to Recognizing Your Personality's Self-limiting Habits)

Mike Houser

Published By Ryan Princeton

Mike Houser

All Rights Reserved

Enneagram: The Complete Guide to Personality Types and Self-discovery Unleash the Empath in You (Effective Steps to Recognizing Your Personality's Self-limiting Habits)

ISBN 978-1-77485-363-4

All rights reserved. No part of this guide may be reproduced in any form without permission in writing from the publisher except in the case of brief quotations embodied in critical articles or reviews.

Legal & Disclaimer

The information contained in this book is not designed to replace or take the place of any form of medicine or professional medical advice. The information in this book has been provided for educational and entertainment purposes only.

The information contained in this book has been compiled from sources deemed reliable, and it is accurate to the best of the Author's knowledge; however, the Author cannot guarantee its accuracy and validity and cannot be held liable for any errors or omissions. Changes are periodically made to this book. You must consult your doctor or get professional medical advice before using any of the suggested remedies, techniques, or information in this book.

Upon using the information contained in this book, you agree to hold harmless the Author from and against any damages, costs, and expenses, including any legal fees potentially resulting from the application of any of the information provided by this guide. This disclaimer applies to any damages or injury caused by the use and application, whether directly or indirectly, of any advice or information presented, whether for breach of contract, tort, negligence, personal injury, criminal intent, or under any other cause of action.

You agree to accept all risks of using the information presented inside this book. You need to consult a professional medical practitioner in order to ensure you are both able and healthy enough to participate in this program.

TABLE OF CONTENTS

INTRODUCTION 1

CHAPTER 1: ABOUT ENNEAGRAM 3

CHAPTER 2: WHAT THE ENNEAGRAM OF PERSONALITY CAN BE UTILIZED BY INDIVIDUALS................................... 12

CHAPTER 3: BUILDING SELF-UNDERSTANDING 32

CHAPTER 4: THE TYPE FOUR PERSONALITY...................... 45

CHAPTER 5: TYPE 3, AND 4 CHARACTERISTICS................. 60

CHAPTER 6: WHAT CAN THE ENNEAGRAM PERSONALITY TYPE BENEFIT YOUR LIFE? 66

CHAPTER 7: THE INVESTIGATOR 74

CHAPTER 8: ENNEAGRAM PERSONALITY TYPE 4 THE ARTIST... 80

CHAPTER 9: 10 SPECIFIC STEPS TO TRANSFORM YOUR LIFE 91

CHAPTER 10: THE ENNEAGRAM TYPES OF PERSONALITY MYTHS & THE FACTS 98

CHAPTER 11: A PERSONA ROAD MAP TEST 106

CHAPTER 12: WARDING OFF YOURSELF FROM UNWANTED EMOTIONS 118

CHAPTER 13: ENNEAGRAM AS A UNIVERSAL SYMBOL OF AN ANCIENT TEACHING... 129

CHAPTER 14: THE THEORY OF ENNEAGRAM.................. 142

CHAPTER 15: ENNEAGRAM TYPE 1: THE PERFECTIONIST 160

CHAPTER 16: TIPS FOR EACH TYPE OF PERSONALITY 171

CHAPTER 17: ESTABLISHING RAPPORT FOR TELEPHONE COACHING... 182

CONCLUSION.. 185

Introduction

In the subsequent chapters we'll take a deep look at the background as well as the significance and method of applying your understanding of the Enneagram to your own life. Learn about the personality types that are part of the Enneagram system, and how to connect with each of them. Everyone is a different type and you'll learn to identify which type you're and also strategies and tricks for cooperating and working with people who belong to different types. There are other factors such as instinctual and wings that can have an impact on your Enneagram types , and you'll be able to learn everything you need to know about yours.

My ultimate goal is that you, my reader - will be able to dive deep into your personality and understand why you behave according to the Enneagram model. I'm confident that it will aid in understanding your personality better and give you a greater insight into your life and the place you are in this world.

To become an Enneagram Master requires processing a vast amount of data. The good news is that this process is already completed "behind an electronic screen" and the pages in this book will provide you with only the most crucial and relevant pieces of information. My aim was to dissect all the important information that you must learn and then present it in an a digestible and easy to comprehend manner.

I hope this book helps you understand the significance and complex nature in the Enneagram system. You will be able to completely and fully integrate your new knowledge in your everyday life.

Chapter 1: About Enneagram

An Enneagram isn't something new In fact, it's been around for quite a long time. It describes nine different types of people. In reality, everyone of us will belong to one of these categories. Simple, isn't that? It's just that simple. The origins of the Enneagram are traced all the way to Middle East, and it can be a valuable instrument to understand human behaviour. The word "enneagram" is a mixture from two Greek words, ennea as well as the word grammos. Ennea is a reference to nine, while the word grammos refers to movement, or something written.

A nine-pointed polygon can be used to represent the Enneagram. In the early 1900s Georgi I. Gurdjieff introduced west to the idea of an Enneagram. He utilized this method to distinguish between the essence of a person and their personality. Oscar Ichazo is known as the founder of the modern version of the Enneagram which we still use. The author wrote his thoughts on it the first time in the 1950s.

The Enneagram is a pseudo-scientific way to determine a person's personality kind. There are nine different types of personality types, and each one is linked to the Enneagram using the aid of lines and fixed points. The connections of the different personality types emerge based on certain established patterns. You may be a part of several personality types however there is only one dominant personality one may have, unless they think you suffer from a disorder that is multi-personal!

Benefits

The main benefit the Enneagram offers is the ability to assist you in understanding your own self. It will assist you to know your inner self. It also helps you understand other people. When you are able to understand others and can become more compassionate to them. The Enneagram will assist you to not only access however, but also increase your mental, emotional and spiritual ability. The

Enneagram will make you aware of your natural reactions and defensive reactions to events that arise in life. If you're conscious of the way that you react and react, you are able to alter your behavior. The only thing you are in control of within your own life are your reaction. The distinction between success and failure is in your response. Your reaction to events can determine the direction in your own life. This is why the Enneagram will increase your effectiveness when dealing with other people. It's not just that it will also help you build lasting connections. It will enable you be present in the moment rather than the past or future. All it boils back to awareness of yourself. Being aware of yourself can enable you to alter your life to the best of your abilities.

Personality Types

The Enneagram is about the core of being. It outlines nine fundamental models of human behavior and each have certain characteristics that are both excellent and undesirable. If you can gain understanding of these types of personalities this will allow you better understand your actions and the behavior of others who are around you. It also can help you to develop your personal growth. Let's take a take a look at these 9 personality kinds.

Typ 1: The Idealionist

Like the name implies an Perfectionist seeks perfection in all aspects. No matter what they are looking to be the best in everything. They are very real, thorough, diligent and adamant. They are usually obsessed with control and insist that everything be flawless. Anything that's not perfect will create an OCD in a Perfectionist (not necessarily). They are disciplined, trustworthy and seek order in their lives. However, they can be irritable demanding, and tend to be very critical of themselves and other people. Stop being a constant critic , and let yourself off the hook!

Type 2. The Helper

Helpers desire to be loved. Of course, they're eager to assist. People who have this type of personality tend to be compassionate. They can be friendly to the point of not being self-aggrandizing. They also find it difficult to say no and often end up in situations easy to avoid. On the other hand they may be annoying or jealous, and can even be possessive. In reality, jealousy and possessiveness are two distinct traits and neither one is ideal. The helpful nature of a helper can cause them to fall.

Type 3 The Achiever

What are they looking for in achievers? They strive to achieve success and achieve it through lots of work. They are extremely positive, energetic, confident and focused. It seems like they're very well-behaved in life does it not? People with this type of personality are extremely efficient and determined. However, they are manipulative, uncooperative and self-centered. Because of these bad attributes, they are often unable to see the feelings of others. It's a race for them, and they would like to win.

Type 4 The Individualist

People who have this type of personality are emotionally driven. They have a strong sense of instinct, but are likely to have a lot of ups and downs throughout life. They aren't happy with monotonous, boring work. The 9-5 work schedule is their worst nightmare. This type of personality can be slightly emotional unstable, and they can exaggerate quite a bit.

The Type 5: The Observer

Observers love to observe, study, and are analytic. They are able to reason about things and not allow their emotions to get the most of them. Also in comparison to other traits of personality they're observant. The drawback of being logical and analytical throughout the day is that they can appear uninterested and aloof.

6. The Loyalist

Loyalists need to be safe and have security. People who have this type of personality are extremely aware of responsibility, and are trustworthy. They adhere to the rules. On the other hand they can be very suspicious and possess the ability to anticipate catastrophes.

Type 7 The Optimist

The primary traits that characterize this type of personality apart from being positive are active and energetic. The optimistic may appear uncontrollable and shallow to some. They often forget about the real world and dwell in their fantasies.

Type 8 The Leader

The leaders of the future aren't born, they're made. This is true technically. However, certain people have the traits of leadership naturally and they belong to this category. The personality type of this kind is self-confident in their independence, direct, and cautious. They aren't afraid of anythingand will not hesitate to engage in conflicts when they are necessary. But, they can appear unwelcome, selfish or even vengeful.

Type 9 The Mediator Mediator

The ninth and last personality type is the Mediator. Mediators are drawn to harmony and unity. They are able to look at an issue in a new way. They are able to see the advantages and disadvantages of every situation. This type of personality is known to be a good negotiator and is a great adapter. On the other hand, mediators tend to get caught up in their own thoughts and may appear to be unfocused. They struggle with prioritizing the things they need to prioritize in their lives.

Enneagram Wings

These nine types of personality listed above are the predominant personality kinds. Beyond that there's something called Enneagram wings. There are nine predominant personality types, and each has its own edge in the polygon. There is a number on either side , which runs along the edges of each of the major figures.

For example The Wings for one are 9 and 2. In the case of Two, there are Three and One. They are called Wings for Three are Two and Four. They are the Wings for Four are Three and Five. Three and Five. Wings for Five are Four and Six. For Six, the Wings for Six are Five and Seven. They are the Wings for Seven are Six and Eight. They are the Wings for Eight are Seven and Nine. They are called the Wings for Nine are Eight and One. If you look at an

Enneagram symbol, you'll be able to quickly identify the pattern. The Enneagram can help you understand your own growth and development. Wings do not alter the dominant characteristics. Instead, they enhance other traits. Wings are also the reason two people who have the same traits have different behavior patterns.

Chapter 2: What the Enneagram Of Personality can be Utilized By Individuals

This chapter will discuss how the enneagram can be utilized by individuals. It will outline ways in that you as an individual could use the diagram, the strengths and weaknesses of every personality. It will describe what strengths and flaws that could be referred to as stress or health of each persona. You can expect that after having read this chapter, you'll be able to utilize the enneagram of your personality to enhance your life and better your life. It is also possible that you are aware of each personality's strength, weakness, and strength. You must also be able recognize and type yourself as well as others after you have read this chapter. The most important thing is that enneagram fundamentals and the rudiments should be understood by everyone who reads this chapter.

As we mentioned earlier, Enneagram as a term is derived from the Greek words of ennea (nine) and gram (a drawn diagram) and is a reference to the nine-sided geometric diagram which provides the foundation for the Enneagram of Personality system which is now widely known. The relationships between these two elements are not obvious, but simultaneously complex, and in actuality too complex to be described at this time, however the essential descriptions of every type are easily grasped.

Being at the core of its existence at its core, the Enneagram offers nine completely diverse ways of responding to or seeing and then acting in the world. The kinds differ from one in a way that they can, without any pressure, be compared to different continents with each having its own unique cosmology, or worldview and a belief system that is completely different from the other.

In contrast to other systems of classification for personalities that are available, the Enneagram tends to concentrate more on the inner functioning system of each person instead of external attributes or characteristics that are easily visible. It lets us consider for a moment what it would be similar to being inside another's mind or their world, and then view the world completely from that. This shift in perception is the basis for an extensive and more profound broad understanding that allows us to assess ourselves more accurately and, at the same time, help us build more satisfying and lasting relationships with each other within our communities.

Consolidating Your Power

According to the theories of the Enneagram, every person has a gift that is natural to them to offer a unique strength distinctive to that type and originates from their internal views of the world. But, as with all strengths it is prone to being misused and then altered to the point that it becomes our biggest vulnerability and weakness. A constant thirst for understanding the inner workings and terrains of your enneagram family (and the other groups) can give you an advantage when it comes to identifying, reassessing the way you compensate and adjust your weaknesses and resolving your negative habits. While doing this it allows you to make the optimal use of the abilities that you have with your unique strengths and capabilities that you've been blessed with in one way or in another. When you are aware of your strengths will make it easy to be able to communicate with other people, and you can stay clear of pitfalls and enhance your life.

In the beginning, you must immediately identify the personality of your spouse, your partners and husband, your best friends as well as your son, daughters, boss your priest and leader, as well as your personal representative, and others from the short descriptions that will be included in this paragraph. If you're unable to find your personality type, I'll suggest that you take a look further into the chapters that follow this chapter. As you continue reading you'll gain an improved understanding of you and your friends. If you are still unable to know yourself, I recommend you to read the chapter again beginning with the introduction and ending with the final chapter. Additionally, what you can expect within this section is that you'll be able to appreciate and gain an understanding of the various alike, but different types of personal and major beliefs which exist. These ideas and beliefs are visible and are displayed by numerous people every day, yet they continue to question why these people behave and react to situations in the way they do. In this chapter, you'll succeed in learning and understand why people behave in the way they do and act how they behave. You might even gain new insights on how to interact more effectively with people you might find offensive, and be a bit confusing with the way they act or respond to various situations.

Let me say that before you continue reading the Enneagram as an idea has a distinct method of engulfing you by engulfing you in a sense and inducing you to seek out more information. I'm sure you'd want to learn more about the enneagram that describes your character, your behavior and the reasons behind why you behave in the way you do. With a myriad of books, journals and courses that are designed to break down the different type of enneagram it's incredibly simple to get hooked on the study of the enneagram. Before you are too thrilled that you're about to master each personality type, I would like to inform you that you'll be in the crosshairs of your peers. Why? Because, very soon you'll be an expert at typing people and at that point you'll find yourself telling people things like: "Oh I see, you're an amazing nine." or "No surprise, you're three." or "Now I'm smarter than you bro, you're a the type two." or "It's okay but I'm not going to blame you because it's not your fault that you're five years old, and that's how you've been programmed and wired to respond to situations." and " Oh my god, you're the perfect child". Are you still in my thoughts? If so, then go through the article because you're about discover the secret to having a completely different persona.

The Nine Types of Enneagram

1. The Perfectionist

Worldview Life is all about striving to develop yourself.

Faiths "Virtue" is not anything other than its own reward for the people who possess it. The people are nothing more than the ideals and principles they believe in. The world could be a wonderful environment if everyone chooses to strive to achieve his best and not wait for the next. They believe that everyone should do our best to become better."

The hardworking and disciplined, perfectionists are always driven by the high internal standards they strive for and are a constant, yet demanding self-criticism. It's possible they assign too many responsibilities to themselves. In addition, because of their ambition, get irritated of the lack of discipline and shortcomings of other people. They also don't like the fact that others who are on the same path and aren't pulling their full weight. While the majority of the world may view perfectionists as a discerning, critical or insatiable humans however, they can be a bit confused and makes them astonished since they are only sharing the smallest fraction of their current internal opinions and opinions. When they are at their most, they're trustworthy, responsible as well as social change-makers. Even at their worst they can be rigid, poor judges and may not be able to adjust to the changes.

2. The Cheerful Giver

Worldview: My love is the sole motor that helps the universe turn.

Believes "I possess a lot of empathy as well as compassion for others. I know what people have always needed and attempt to help them, without weighing the price and what it will cost me. The mind of the person giving the gift; it is also an idea that I am extremely valuable to my family, friends employers customers, siblings and even my son."

Warm and caring, they love to bless others and nurture them to full development and growth. They are also known for their ability to network because they create real connections between people. It is however, sad that they are so focused on the demands of others that they neglect themselves, and exhaust themselves of all their energy, and then become lost. They also get overwhelmed when they observe the needs of others and may become frustrated when they realize the needs of other people aren't being met by those who have to be attending to their demands. When they are at their most, they're generous and could be described as being altruists by the sense of their nature. In their worst moments they could manipulate their generosity and may "give to get."

3. The Performers Who Really Are

Worldviews The most important thing in life is to be as a successful human being more than any other thing.

Beliefs: "Yes, I am my own achievements, and I have to change to the changing circumstances that surround me. They believe that everyone is looking to be seen as winners. Therefore, they should be striving to become an individual winner according to their own personal way."

They are multitaskers, extremely high-energy individuals, and are known as focused and ambitious people. They are able to quickly adjust to any setting of any kind or group in such a short time that they can meet their current surroundings with incredible ease. The focus is on the achievement of their goals, that can cause them to put other areas of their lives in a bind. This is due to the fact that they are extremely adept at selling their personalities, themselves as well as their goals and goals to other people. People who perform can feel like they've done nothing wrong, but have fabricated their accomplishments in certain ways. At their top, they are an enthralling go-getter, achiever and focused. When they are at their lowest they are known to be self-promotional and a dazzling people who work hard.

4. The Real Romantic

Worldviews: They are able to see the perspective that something vital is missing from life , and it is in need of getting.

The beliefs that define me "I completely different to everyone else around me. Nobody can fully understand me, no matter how hard they try to. True authenticity, as a concept is something that is only discovered in profound emotions."

Romantics always seek out of emotional connections and the depth. They have the capacity to feel present in the most difficult situations in life, such as loss, depression, grief and death and serve as a role an example for other people or people who be able to endure the most difficult times of their lives. Romantics also shine their light on the riches that can be discovered in the course of life. They are unique, imaginative and creative in every endeavor they encounter. They have numerous creative talents and have a keen sense of appreciation and of the aesthetic. They always have the aim of making an exceptional contribution to the world and provide a valuable to those who surround them. At their finest, Romantics are so sensitive and extremely genuine. In their worst moments they could be emotional and moody even but there's no reason to be.

5. The True Observer

Worldviews Life is a constant search for wisdom, knowledge and understanding.

Believes "People as well as other things can be overwhelming and drain your energy. This can leave you exhausted. They believe that knowledge is the only power that needs to be sought."

Observers are able to separate themselves from emotions and needs, biases as well as the opinions of others. The ability to be cool and clear and calm as well as self-control are the norm for them in circumstances that others struggle to handle in an uncontrollable situation. They are extremely independent, self-contained and self-sustaining individuals. They also have an extremely developed capacity for understanding, analyzing, and synthesizing complex and complex situations, data and hostile environments. But, they can also appear too egocentric and smug when a more empathetic approach is essential to maintain the situation. The need for privacy is a major factor that can lead to the self-deprivation or isolation. Sometimes, observers appear distant , or emotionally inaccessible and disconnected, and when under stress they might stifle the energy, feelings and even their attention from all things.

6. The Chronic Skeptic

They are considered to be people who have the highest loyalty or are loyalists.

Worldviews: The globe is a hazardous and risky location to live in.

Credos "Always anticipate the worst in any situation. If you make a plan for the most likely scenario that might be the case, then you'll protect yourself from danger. Don't take any risk, no matter the fascinating aspect, on the surface, since there's always something unique in every situation."

Skeptics, sometimes called loyalists, possess a wide range of capabilities of imagination and creative thinking. They are able to recognize the negative effects, risks incompatibilities, dangers, or dangers that are inherent in any situation in which they are confronted with. They are skilled and deft planners who think about the final outcome from the beginning. Skeptics can masterly envision ways in how they can handle risks or avoid any danger that comes with the scenario they're in. While they constantly fear the worst that can occur to them, if the worst of their fears actually happens to them, skeptical people quickly move to other options and often display incredible bravery, courage and unimaginable courage. Their extremely sophisticated sense of danger could be activated at times when the danger is not even the most extreme. Other types of enneagrams might think that skeptics are people who preach destruction, doom and gloom or even excessive danger and uncontrollable worry and agitation. When they are at their best they can be skilled problem solvers who can find solutions to any problem or issue. In the worst case they could become doubtful Thomas as well as be prone to over-analyzing situations. They can have a difficult time deciding to act since they tend to consider the risks inherent in each scenario; they may also be too egocentric and pessimistic.

7. The Real Positives
Perspectives on Life: It's an adventure filled with endless possibilities one can explore.
Believes "Life can be more than experiencing the world and it's about having any experiences you can have. The options available in a variety of forms are endless. Shutting down any option is like being into a trap without being able to escape from the trap."
The optimists are referred to as positive-energy, positive vibe and optimistic people They can wrap others in their excitement even when people are reluctant to take action. They are great and are known for their big ideas and lofty opinions. They are also a values-oriented group of individuals,

who continuously crank out endless ideas, possibilities and possibilities that can be fully tapped. Concentrating on the positive side of any circumstance can enable them to avoid and overcome difficulties or pain that is easily observed and manageable in any circumstance. Others or groups of people may believe that optimists are a type who cannot be trusted during times of hardship and chaos. They're thought to not prepared to confront important and pressing issues that must be dealt with. The feeling of being shackled by a lack of options that might not permit them to think about alternatives may also create issues with loyalty to groups, individuals, or cause, tasks , or the ideology. When they are at their most optimists are believed as fun-loving visionaries and revolutionary. In their worst, they are often an unfocused person who is entangled in the vision that is being promoted however they do not have any serious plans or information that could aid them in securing their goals.

8. The Boss Identified

Worldviews: The universe we inhabit is a wild animal habitat. Each man is there for himself. Only those who are strong can survive in the wilderness.

The beliefs "The reality can only be discovered in honest (even even if it's unfair) fights. Life is meant to be lived in a way that is reckless, passionately and with a passion that is not kept back, but within my own terms. I must guard my part of the world, lest someone else steals it away."

Straight-shooters are also considered to be the boss who is not concerned about the interests of others than their own. They are such a decisive, straightforward with nothing held back, what-you-actually-see-is-what-you eventually-get kind of people. They have full control and take decisions swiftly without any delay. They are known as individuals of action, who inspire others with only the force of their willpower. Straight-shooters are frequently regarded as protectors of the less strong, weak, and ineffective as well as the advocates of social justice. They are the cerebral confident, classical and bigger-than-life kind of leaders. They offer more than 100 percent of everything they get their hands on. They are often abrupt, impetuous, pushy, and even reactionary. Their decisions tend fast-moving through gut instinct, whereas the natural instinct might not be enough. They are not concerned about feelings or thoughts of conflict when making decisions. When they are at their best they are so powerful and a protector of their domain. When they are at their worst they're steam-rolling bosses who are apprehensive about bossing everyone else around.

9. The True Mediator

The worldview: It's all about harmony, but also about moving with the flow.

Beliefs: "Having one's own view and agenda, beliefs, or opinions that differ from the rest of the world could disrupt the peace that is prevalent in the world. Therefore it's more important and incredibly beneficial to go with the flow and remain in harmony with the rest of humanity. In the true sense of the word there is nothing that matters at all in the world that we live in. Conflict should be avoided at all cost, regardless of what might be lost. What can be gained by working in harmony is more than what is lost.

Mediators are believed to be the most discerning recipients of the Enneagram of Personality: They are very open and tolerant of the opinions of others without making any judgements about them. They are able to detect the internal state of anotherwhether they are in a calm state or one that is chaotic and strive to accept people for who they are without judgement. They are able to sync with the state of other people's mind. Through this understanding and understanding are the ability to recognize all the different and divergent perspectives of a specific problem, which ultimately helps them become peace-makers between conflicting group or faction. But being able to view the entire spectrum of an issue can make it difficult for them to make a decision or prioritize choices in the time. The mediator's insatiable desire for peace, tranquility and harmony may hinder the possibility of a complete improvement in healthy conflict, constructive critics, healthy competition and problem-solving abilities. Continuously moving with the flow and blending with other's agendas makes it that they are unable to discern their own desires and separate them from demands of the group. They lack genuine goals and individual views. In their most effective form Mediators are said as constant peacemakers accepting people for who they are without condemning them. In their worst moments they're apathetic people who are apathetic and lack ambitions or their own voice.

Chapter 3: Building Self-Understanding

"Who is me?" This is an ancient question. How many have answered the question themselves in truthfulness? This chapter will explore the psychology component of understanding the personality. Self-understanding is defined by the dictionary to mean "awareness of and the ability to comprehend one's own behavior and responses." There are a lot of people are wondering what it means to understand themselves. We are surrounded by designations and titles: mother, athlete or singer, married single, married. Why do we need to learn anything more? If we believe that we're able to live happily in our daily lives, then why bother is it? What is the point of tackling the more emotional, uncomfortable aspect of our identity?

Why is self-understanding so important? Understanding ourselves can help us recognize our uniqueness. We aren't just a part of those around us once we are aware of what we think, how we feel and what makes us happy or sad. We find out what our weaknesses lie, and then learn to adjust and accept the inevitable changes that come with our ever-changing world. Self-awareness shows us what we are familiar with and what we are still able to find out. So, often, we seek to hide the flaws in us, which may make them appear more evident to others.

In order to better be able to better understand ourselves Let's glance at the concept of "self" is according to popular psychological theories.

What exactly is "Self"?

"Self" can be described as a term with many facets. There is the physical aspect which is the amount of activity we do, the things we love to do with our spare time, and our favourite sports, or activities. The social side: how we interact with others and whether we prefer to be in large groups or with a few people or by ourselves in our own space, how much we become acquainted with people. The competence aspect: how well to look after ourselves, maintain a job and pay rent, regardless of regardless of whether we look after our families or ourselves to take care of, and our ability to accomplish the tasks.

Other important aspects of self-knowledge are self-esteem, self-perception and self-awareness.

Self-Knowledge

The process of learning about yourself is based upon a question that is its own "what is my personality?" It is not just the information we have about ourselves, but also our need to find knowledge which leads to a better knowledge of the concept of self. It's an image of ourselves that we create in our minds about our individuality. Individuality is composed of many characteristics that we associate with us as we identify the attributes that we have in common. Self-knowledge can be found in the realm of cognition self. It is the things we know about ourselves as well as what we believe we have a good idea of. This is a reference to physical characteristics of an individual like ethnicity and eye color, and body structure and more psychological aspects like morals and convictions.

Self-Perception

Perception is described as "a method of evaluating an understanding, understanding, or interpretation the mental impression." Daryl Bem, psychologist, has proposed self-perception with regard to the formation of attitudes. Bem says that humans naturally form attitudes in response to uncertain or unexperienced situations. This is done because we are aware of what we do and then acting accordingly to an event. This concept has been perceived as contradictory, but some believe that it's not our behavior that defines our behaviour, but it is our attitudes as a whole that affect the way we behave. The most effective way to look at self-perception is to look at possibilities that might take a different direction. If we look at the final part that defines perception it boils down to the same aspect that is understanding. If self-knowledge is the process of gathering information about us and our environment, then self-perception refers to the ability to process the information. We then can be aware of the reasons why we react and respond to certain events in the way that we respond to them.

Self-Esteem

Self-esteem can be understood on a personal level. It is a reflection of the longing part of our personality. It's the way we perceive ourselves and our perception of our worthiness, whether that's the way other people perceive ourselves or otherwise. Self-esteem is an entirely subjective thing and may be either positive or negative. Certain people do not just consider themselves to be capable, desirable, worthy and valued, but they may believe that too. Some people want to be a part of all these beliefs and have them validated by others, but not be able to accept them, or even see them in their own eyes. It is more typical for us to believe in the negative self-talk. Many people who suffer from low self-esteem believe that they are not attractive, worthy or unworthy. Self-esteem is a crucial factor in how we live our lives. It influences the outcome of our work, how we handle family and other social relationships, and even the outcomes of academic endeavors.

Self-Awareness

Self-awareness is the capacity to realize that we are unique person, separate from anyone other. This is the way to be aware of our personalities and our personality that includes our feelings and motivations, as well as our preferences and dislikes. Self-awareness can be divided into two parts both internal and external. External awareness is naturally conscious of our body's condition in relation to the human condition, health and the external interpretation of the internal sensations. In this book, we're mostly interested in our inner awareness that is our emotional reactions. A key part of understanding our own self is to be mindful of emotions we're experiencing and the triggers that cause the emotions to manifest.

Jungian Self Archetype

Carl Jung has produced many useful theories about self and personality. The well-known Myers-Briggs personality test is based on his theories of introverted and extroverted personality types. Jung believed there were two levels in our subconscious mind: the collective and personal. Evolution is a major factor in this view and argues that there exists an "collective" instinctual thinking and process that has evolved across all of us over hundreds of years of development. He classified these ancient habits in "archetypes." According to them, they were the basis of every social practice regardless of where, when or to who the person was born. A man who is wealthy living in the city could exhibit the same behavior like an Ecuadorian native who lives in a hut within the forest. There's a much more extensive list of 12 archetypes Jung identified. They are derived from four primary ones: Shadow, Anima and Animus,

Persona, and Self. The Jungian theory says that Self is the center of the entire personality--including the unconscious, the conscious, and the ego. It is typically represented by the form of a circle because it symbolizes the entire psychological system. He asserts that Self isn't just the most important archetype, but it is also a difficult concept to grasp. He believed that it was an individual entity and that is the source for our dreams, and he believed that a complete understanding of the real Self is impossible. The theory of his was that, in the initial "phase" in our life we are created into the "primal" conscious. As we get older and become more mature, we develop our individual personalities, our personal "self." The method is complicated and can be a bit complicated. It's more psychological than we'll ever need to be able to use however, one thing that remains is that the self is crucial and understanding what we're about is the first step towards understanding who we are.

Johari Window

Another method for figuring out ourselves is known as "the Johari Window. It was invented by two psychologists, Harrington Ingram and Joseph Luft. Johari Window Johari Window gives us four fundamental types of the Self that are: obscure, known and blind.

The hidden self is the part of us that we see and feel about our own self that we don't want to be seen and that others do not. It is where we conceal certain aspects of ourselves that aren't willing to reveal. It's very private and secure because of a variety of reasons. This is the kind of thing we are likely to feel ashamed or guilty of, or be afraid to show vulnerability. The self that is hidden could show good qualities of modesty and humility.

In contrast, the self we know is the aspect we are visible by the rest of humanity. It's both what we see as well as what others around us see. We are able to share our personal self freely with others and are able to be at peace to the way we have defined this part of us to be.

The unidentified self is somewhat more obscure. It's the part which neither outside world or we are able to see. It can refer to both positive and negative things we haven't even thought about at the moment. It can also be a sign of undiscovered abilities or possibilities; things we haven't uncovered about ourselves. Discovering the inner self isn't easy. It requires stepping out of our comfort zones, accepting the change, and trying out new ways of doing things.

Then, there's the self that is blind. It is the aspect of us that is not visible from us but recognized by others in our lives. It also exposes the our beliefs about who we consider our self-image to be. Many people believe that they're organized and focused and organized, but others might disagree. We may be caught over the belief that we're not capable or have particular skills, while others might be completely different. One of the most effective ways to develop self-understanding as well as awareness is to receive feedback from those in our lives.

This means being able to consider both the positive and the negative about our own lives, but it's an excellent activity to take into consideration.

Understanding Self and the Enneagram

Now that we have a better understanding about the concept of "self" is, it's time to consider ways that using the Enneagram model can aid in understanding ourselves. Step one is simple to Take the Enneagram test to determine your personality. The next step could be more challenging: be open-minded and take the bad alongside the positive.

One of the greatest obstacles in gaining this type of knowledge in depth is fear. Fear keeps us locked in our places Fear of failure or not being able to measure with others, fear of not being accepted The list of reasons could be endless. The misuse or misuse of the Enneagram tool can cause more anger and fear than it was intended to, but a sensible method of self-evaluation could yield excellent outcomes.

Everyone should strive to be more than we are, and that's one of the primary motives to attempt to improve your self-knowledge. That's the main goal that is the primary goal of this Enneagram model. Although there are negatives to every person, the Enneagram highlights how each person excels and shines. Before you take the Enneagram test However, it might be beneficial to ask a few specific questions to yourself. Questions such as: What three words would I choose to describe my personality? What are my three or two strongest strengths? What would be my weaknesses? What would I like to improve about myself? If I answer these questions as truthfully as you can will make identifying as an Enneagram type a little more straightforward.

Everyone has gifts and potential. We each have something valuable to contribute in every aspect in our life. It is not wise to judge each of these nine people as bad or good. All of them have positive qualities and each have their own blind spots. The Enneagram is already able to identify the most important areas of potential blind spots in every type of personality. Once we've identified our personal identity, the first step of self-understanding involves accepting the blind spots, and then working on the blind spots.

Chapter 4: The Type Four Personality

Type Four (individualist and romantic) A person who is an individualist one, the Type Four personality wants to establish their distinct identity, and be a significant person rather than an ordinary passer-by. They might be unable to adjust to a world that is controlled by a set of rules. A romantic, Type Four is a supportive emotional, passionate, and compassionate being. They get their self-worth and self-esteem through their relationships.

The features of Type Fours are : These are the characteristics of Type Fours:

* Individuals who have Type Four personality traits are sensitive to what other people suffer and will offer assistance in any way they can. They are able to spot issues that other people overlook, which is why they possess the ability to analyze an issue and determine its root cause. They are devoted to helping others , even if they have any immediate benefits or gains. They see the benefits of relationships as a currency that can be exchanged to obtain whatever they want , even though there isn't any return currently.

* The Type Four personality types are looking for something that they may not more value as they ought to when they are able to have it. Their spouses could be unable to appreciate their personality because they are difficult to be pleasing to. Therefore, it is best to put off their satisfaction in the relationship to them.

Type Fours tend in blaming themselves for their mistakes regardless of the fact that other causes are to the blame. They believe that there's some thing they should have done differently to improve the circumstances they are in. The ability to have an internal source of control may allow individuals to resolve certain problems within their lives without requiring assistance from other people.

Type Fours have an intense admiration for famous people and those with authority who appear to be unique in them. This is why they are attracted to bizarre personalities such as radical feminists, rock stars with eccentricities and magicians, rebels as well as survivalists and on. They don't realize it but they might view them as role models, and in certain cases even as idols.

* Type Fours draw their energy from others and are influenced by the way their perceptions are received. By what they contribute to others and being part of an emotional circle, their opinions as well as those of their closest friends are important to them. They are part of a small circle of friends that are important to them. In the absence of this circle, they may not be paying attention to the way that the world is thinking or feeling about them.

* Type Fours are used to living an eccentric lifestyle and often show this type of way of life in their everyday habits. They could be vegetarians or continue to use the same vehicle or home for a long period of time, in the event that it is satisfying their requirements. They are often very deep in their beliefs and way of life. It's not uncommon to observe people of the

Type Four asking questions about the significance and meaning of the universe. Being philosophical may help boost their energy levels elevated when they debate or discuss these issues in life.

* Their views most of the time are a bit different and this is a problem for them little. They know that there are going to be other people in the world who have similar opinions on the same topic or subject. They could live their entire life fighting for the protection of animal rights, the inclusion of financial resources for the socially marginalized and even for the defense of LGBT rights within the communities in which they live and work.

* Type Fours are known to daydream about the future or becoming lost on the past. Once they've got an understanding of what they want to see (whether within their own lives, families, or even a nation) they can start to envision the future coming into being and this could continue for years without others around them not even noticing the idea. The same thing could occur with regard to the past, as

they may be attempting to change the narratives of the past in their mind.

Below are some examples of the most famous "Type Four" personalities from the history of humanity --

* Francis Bacon - An English statesman, philosopher and scientist who was Attorney General as well as Lord Chancellor for England. Bacon is often referred to as the founder of empirical thinking because his work had a profound impact on the advancement in the science method in the revolution in science. As a Type Four the man he was described as having three goals: to find the truth, to serve his country, and help the Church. He sought to achieve this goal by pursuing the highest position. As per his personal secretary, chaplain and personal assistant Francis Bacon was always tender-hearted and was not a victim of violence, and didn't seek do anything to hurt or discredit anyone else.

* Marlon Brando, an American actor and director of films who had a significant influence on the film industry during the

latter half of the century. Brando had a variety of performances that won awards in movies during three decades, and was active in various causes, including Civil Rights movements. The Type Four personality may have been reinforced during his early years, which were marked by the lack of affection and love from his father, who often told that he couldn't achieve anything and that he would have no value. He grew up hoping to be loved and felt special.

* Michael Jackson - An American dancer and singer often described as"the King" of Pop. He is among the most well-known entertainers in the world, and among the top-selling artists ever His contribution to fashion, music and dance as well as his public life has have made him a prominent celebrity in pop culture for more than four years. Michael Jackson's Type Four personality was reinforced by a difficult childhood, which Michael Jackson believes is not real. Michael Jackson stated that he was physically and emotionally assaulted throughout his endless rehearsals. He also

credited the strict discipline of his father for being a significant factor in his career. The deep discontent he felt about his appearance and habit of being a perfectionist and to be a childlike adulthood is consistent with the consequences of the abuse he experienced when he was a kid.

* Prince Charles of Wales The eldest child from Queen Elizabeth II, and the likely heir of the British throne. He has served as the Duke of Cornwall and Duke of Rothesay since 1952. He is the longest-serving and oldest successor apparent to the British throne in British history. Prince Charles has shattered a lot of traditional royal practices in his efforts to be unique. Prince Charles was the very first royal heir apparent who attended school within walls of a formal school, rather than being taught by an individual tutor. He also chose to go to university instead of joining in the British Armed Forces right following high school. This was an exception from the traditional British the royal family.

* Vincent Van Gogh - A Dutch painter, who is one of the most well-known and influential people within the world of Western art. In just a little over 10 years, he produced around 2,100 pieces of art comprising 860 oil paintings majority of which were created during the latter two decades of his career. His paintings included landscapes, still-life portraits, as well as self-portraits with bold colours and expressive brushwork that created the basis for contemporary art. Vincent Van Gogh was a classic Type Four. He had a poor time in existence and was thought of as to be a liar and an unqualified failure. He gained fame after his suicide, and is remembered in the popular imagination as the most under-appreciated art and genius.

* Nicholas Cage - An American actor director, producer, and actor who has won awards for his acting and writing ability. These are the Academy Award, Golden Globe Award and the Screen Actors Guild Award. Being a Type Four, He is a person who does things in his own style. In the

absence of realizing that at the beginning that he began his acting career, the actor was able to create his own unique acting style , which he refers to as "Nouveau Shamanic. He is drawn to characters with a grotesque look and is praised for his wild and uncontrolled approach to these characters. He is said to be the only actor after Marlon Brando to have created anything unique in the art of film-acting as a result of his ability to steer the film audience away from their obsession with naturalism to a different kind of style of presentation that was well-liked by troubadours. When he was a child, Michelangelo was sent to learn grammar in Florence however, he did not show any desire to attend school and preferred to copy paintings from churches and to seek his fellow artists.

* Michelangelo A.K.A. Michelangelo, an Italian painter, sculptor poet, and architect who had a profound impact on the development of western art. He is regarded as among the most important art

historians of his time. He is often referred to as the ideal Renaissance man. The most well-documented artist of the 16th century certain of his works of sculpture, painting and architecture are as some of the most well-known ever created. He led a very frugal life , and he wanted to do almost everything with moderation, regardless of amount of money or resources available to him. He was naturally one of a lonely and solitary person who was fond of removing himself from social gatherings with males.

* Edgar Allan Poe - An American editor, writer and literary critic, who is most well recognized for his short stories. His work influenced literature in both the United States and around the world, and appear all over popular culture through film, literature, music and on television. Also, he played an important role in the creation of literary genres such as science fiction and detective stories. As a foster kid He was a mix of disobedient and scolding by his parents. This could have led to that Type Four trait to be reinforced

later on. He is considered to be the first famous American writer to make a living writing on his own.

The most common roles played by Type Fours are the following:

* The Maverick The typical Four-person person can be described as an individualist who's not scared to swim against the current. When they face something, they consider it in a clear and rational manner before deciding on a side or even doing take a stand at all. While the majority of people belong to one party or another however, they are able to choose not to join one of them and instead decide on a position based upon the political orientations or preferences.

* The Outsider Type Fours are not afraid to separate themselves from groups from a psychological perspective in the event that they feel that the values and the orientation of the group do not coincide with their own. They will not usually show unanimity or alignment to please a person or group. Their opinions on issues are important to them greatly.

* The Misfit Type Fours might be the odd man or woman within a group particularly when they're not conformity with the established norms and rules. When viewed with negative connotations, they can be a significant source of trouble in the community as they might commit crimes they justification within their own minds.

* The Connoisseur Type Four person could develop their skills and abilities to extremely high levels, making them experts in their particular area of interest. They are focused in achieving a specific job or discipline, and they can effortlessly accomplish what other people consider difficult to achieve.

* The Bohemian is a Bohemian is typically an artist or intellectual who has an unconventional lifestyle . You will not be able to find a better match than an individual who is a Type Four. No matter if they receive the Nobel Prize for science or literature, they are completely committed to their work, and this work is often rooted in roots in the way they perceive the world.

* The poet in the garret. A garret is a part of a home which is located under the roof or in the attic. As a poet in the garret Type Fours prefer working on their own instead of working in teams. They thrive in solitude, as it allows them to discover their talents and imagination. Being in a calm setting helps them stay productive.

"The self-destructive" genius If taken to an extreme, they may start to create false perceptions of reality. Thus, their thoughts or outputs could be further than reality and might not be relevant or useful. Sometimes, they require a continuous review of their own reality and the inputs of others to yield acceptable outcomes.

* The spurned lover Type Fours might not be concerned about the opinions and attention of everyone, except for those they consider to be a big deal to them. When those people don't pay any attention or disagree with their views, it can be extremely demoralizing for them. The rejection of their views can make them be depressed or moody.

* The Aristocrat Type Fours are able to live an organized life which gives an air of nobility surrounding them. They are recognized for their refusal to take pleasure in order to achieve this. The discipline they need is natural to them and once they are ensconced in an established routine or habit, they are unable to break it.

* The Loner Type Fours might not be particularly social, but time spent alone is an awful lot for them. They will do everything they can to have the time with their loved ones, regardless of what schedule they are on. Being in a relationship alone can also mean into time spent with friends of the circle of friends with whom they are most at ease.

Type Fours are those who have an unrelenting desire to stand out in every aspect of their lives, including thoughts, appearance, opinions and routines. They don't want to be a part of the mold that is made by society. Being different from other people gives them a sense of fulfillment and they are more comfortable with only a small portion of the group, rather than the whole group. They may not be able to adhere to specific rules and regulations, but they could make significant contributions to the group in terms of innovation and originality. On the plus side, they could be helpful and intuitive, as well as skilled, compassionate, and innovative. On the flip side they are often obstinate moralistic, guilt-ridden introverted and self-conscious.

Chapter 5: Type 3, and 4 Characteristics

Synopsis

The top performers are those who seek the praise of their peers. They love being in the spotlight and will do anything to succeed, gain fame, wealth, or anything that gets an attention from the peers. They are hard-working, competitive seeking, and awed by the high performance and rewards such as the highest sales, top division, or even the best score in an online game.

A person who is unique, the individualist enjoys being different from all other humanity. They are extremely conscious of their uniqueness and possess unlimited creativity due to the fact that they are unique from other people. They are averse to the ordinary routine, monotony and everything that is typical. Analysers and deep thinkers they can be described as the philosophers of our times and have a keen desire to be involved in the arts even if they don't end up becoming artists.

Type 3 Characteristics: Performer Motivator, Achiever Status Seeker or Producer

They also exude a sense of extroversion, possess a high level of energy due to their way of presenting themselves. They love their image of success and never ever give up, lest they be called a loser. The chameleon is often the most common type, and they are sometimes portrayed as fake particularly when their main focus of vanity and idol worship manifests. They struggle to differentiate their own identity from that of a human and a 'human'.

It's not a surprise that their primary focus is to believe in hope. They're constantly launching new projects motivated by the desire to accomplish or "catch" something fresh. Once one project is completed they are hoping to accomplish something new with their next project.

The biggest fear of people is that they will be unworthy and the inability to perform in a situation.

They are motivated to provide worth to others since they usually define their own importance in the context of awards and acclaim.

The biggest temptation for them is to please everyone. Since their lives are shaped by the expectations of society, others or the pursuit of success society, they often alter who they really are by becoming robotic and apathetic as they go about their quest.

Their biggest sin is deceit. This does not mean that they are outright lying but rather that they are the one who will be immersed in the character they are performing to achieve a specific outcome. This means that their human doing side of them is so intense that the actor is transformed into the person they are playing.

The most successful perform best when they are real and honest with themselves, recognizing their deepest needs and restoring their hopes.

Types threes that have wings of two are known to be very adorable and helpful.

They want to be like the perfect partner, parent or best friend. Type Threes with an four-sided wing are usually less self-conscious, but they could have an illusion of grandeur and are more interested in artistic outcomes.

Type 4 Characteristics: Individualist Artist, Over-Analyzer mystic, or Melodramatic Elitist

They are visually sensitive extremely romantic, and they enjoy everything that is self-expression discovery or self-discovery... frequently sharing their discoveries with others and making a huge contributions to humanity. They are also extremely moody and reserved individuals particularly when their primary focus of sadness is apparent.

Their main goal is to discover the source of their identity. They are those who are never satisfied until they realize their true self. They often go deep into their feelings to discover more about themselves.

Their biggest fear is appearing normal. They are averse to the ordinary routine, the mundane and the routine, and prefer to be different from the rest of us.

They seek authenticity and individuality. They'll take any step to feel unique and unique and want genuine and honest interactions with other people - usually disliking fakery.

Their most enticing temptation is self-castigation and withdrawal. If they feel unsatisfied or having a problem they are likely to constantly blame themselves and shut off from the threatening external world.

The most dreaded vice of them is envy, as they always want the same things as others, believing about how their life is complete or perfect (due to the belief that they're never truly complete).

They're at their peak when they master the art of calmness by accepting the power of present moment and embracing the present... taking in every single moment.

Type fours that have a wing of three are typically more aristocratic forms of elite - the more extrovert of the individualist type when fours with a wings of fives tend to be more reserved complicated, scholarly, and surrounded by the private mythology of loss and pain.

Chapter 6: What Can the Enneagram Personality Type Benefit Your Life?

After you've learned more about the significance behind various personalities, you're thinking about how this information can assist you. The goal of knowing the personality type of your character is to find your own inner mechanism, comprehend the internal mechanisms that constantly change or grow in all aspects that you live.

What can Enneagram aid me in my development?

Enneagram is the key to personal growth and self-discovery through awareness. In this book, as we'll discuss the personality of an Enneagram is identified by inner patterns i.e. those that relate to your thoughts, motivations and the ways in which you react to various situations. Sometimes , we don't realize these patterns since they appear natural to us. Here's the point where Enneagram comes in. It offers a comprehensive analysis of your personality and aids you in becoming conscious of your feelings as well as your needs and thoughts.

The ability to recognize is essential for making changes. If you're not aware of your habits that are automatic and predictable and the impact they have upon your lifestyle, how will you know what needs to be changed and what to do? With a thorough analysis of your mind and all aspects of your personality The Enneagram helps you identify what your weaknesses and strengths are. This way, you will know the areas you need to improve to achieve success and be happier or meet a specific target. That's how you can grow and progress regularly.

The type of your personality on the Enneagram will reveal the areas where you are most likely to get "stuck" or identifies the most typical struggles you encounter along with your anxieties. In essence, it exposes all the mechanisms that motivate you, making it easier to comprehend your own inner patterns. Through the Enneagram it's much easy to comprehend why we encounter certain difficulties however, in the same way you're better equipped to conquer these difficulties. If, for instance, you're unable to let go of bad experiences in the past, it might be easier if you understand the nature of your Enneagram. How? It reveals why you feel this way, and instead of denial of your feelings and stifling your feelings, you gain empathy for yourself. Understanding the reasons behind your emotions both negative and positive can help you process emotions in a healthy way. This is another way the Enneagram assists you grow.

Perhaps the most significant benefit of the Enneagram in self-development is its impartiality. The personality of your character has strengths and weaknesses. Everyone has their flaws and it's impossible to be flawless. But, at times, we don't have the right perspective and tend to judge ourselves too often. In addition, you may appear to be an arrogant or intimidating person although that's not your intention. Being misinterpreted is a typical event and doesn't solely depend on how other people perceive of us. It is also a result of how you view yourself and others. The Enneagram can help you gain an in-depth understanding of your personality in a objective way. It helps you become aware of your strengths and weaknesses and this is an excellent method to develop into an empathetic loved, successful, and loving person, or to reach your goals.

Some people are confident and have learned the art of loving themselves some weren't. The biggest obstacle that stops us from achieving our goals is the lack of self-love. Enneagram is a solution to this issue too. Through understanding, you can have a passion for something and your persona isn't an exception. The more you learn about yourself and your inner thoughts that are entangled with thoughts, feelings and relationships, the simpler it becomes to cultivate self-love.

The Enneagram also urges you to take part in every aspect of your life. What is this implying? Sometimes we're in a state of passiveness and believe that things will just happen or we're fearful of failure, and it's logical to sit back and wait to wait to see what happens. But life doesn't work this way. Each person creates their own happiness and success. Every type of personality achieves success in a different manner dependent on their own internal patterns. However, Enneagram will encourage everyone (regardless of your type) to act and enhance your capacity to live a happy and harmonious life. In this case, the word harmonious could mean something completely distinct for every person However, the main point is that instead of sitting still and wait for events to occur and you are more active. With the capacity to attain that goal you have the opportunity to develop and attain your ideal self-image.

Many ways to identify your what type of personality you have can help improve your quality of life

The Enneagram reveals a person's personality, allowing us to observe the inner structures. Because we can identify the strengths as well as weaknesses in a person, they are given the opportunity to improve in every aspect of our life. If you're wondering whether you can enhance your life by taking advantage of your personality type, this can help you. There are a variety of ways that you can enhance your life simply by determining whether you're Type One Five, Six or another:

Adopting the fullness of your self What you can learn from the Enneagram can teach you is that your entire personality is interconnected. It is impossible to believe in your strengths without knowing your weaknesses. If you are aware of your character type, it becomes easier to accept your true self.

* Helps to narrow your focus - you're drawn to things that fit your personality most. Sometimes, we get lost and can be difficult to pinpoint a real passion. A particular personality type is a key element that determines each person and helps you to understand the things you'd like to accomplish or experience.

* You're not alone . we are part of more than eight billion people around the world and we all feel lonely at times. We go through good and bad moments have failed and succeeded Love and long to love, yet there comes a point that you feel as if no one can understand you. When you read the descriptions of your personality (or another person's) you feel a feeling of belonging, and also realize that you're not the only one. There are many others who are experiencing the same issues.

Being less critical The best thing about the world is the diversity it offers and diversity, we've all judged others for not thinking or act in the way we would. If you want to conceal it, the right option is to recognize it and figure out a solution to resolve the issue. The Enneagram personality type can help to accomplish this. Understanding your type of personality is an excellent method to know your character and how you are able to judge other people. While doing so knowing about the different types will help you be aware of their motivations and are less prone to judgment when you think about a topic in their eyes.

* Helps you believe in your own self-confidence - we've all heard numerous suggestions and tips to lead a happier life. Although there is no problem with them suggestions, it's the time to acknowledge that the one size fits all approach isn't applicable in this case. Different people require a unique approach to everything in life. This is why it's crucial to believe in yourself and in your capacity to achieve amazing things in your life. The personality type of your character helps you sort the advice of others based on your own values. This way, you can take what you can from other people, but remain loyal to yourself in the process

Chapter 7: The Investigator

Fives are both intense and intelligent. They can be insightful and ingenuous. However, they may be also private and isolating.

Fives are intelligent and curious. They are also aware. They love solving mental puzzles. Fives are inventive and creative However, they are more in their own world. They are often lost in their thoughts, pondering ideas.

While remaining disconnected from society Fives are often high-strung and passionate. They are prone to problems with eccentricity, nihilism and a sense of isolation. In many cases, they put too much attention on the academic side of things. They do not develop practical and social skills.

Positively, Fives are visionary pioneers. They are regarded as "ahead by a generation" because they possess the ability to view the world and the situations they face in a distinctive way. Fives aren't turned off by the tried and tested. Instead, they would like to be the ones to find new territory, and have the distinction of being the first one to discover what's new. Many Fives will identify a particular area they believe they have the ability to be a master of.

Fives are driven to study all they can about the world around them.

They plan everything and utilize expertise to guard themselves against unexpected setbacks.

Fives worry about being useless They develop their capacity to think of innovative solutions to complex issues. They don't believe that they have a unique skill to contribute. They use their knowledge of research to develop new skillsso that they have something valuable to offer in the global community. They might use their expertise and experiences to come up with something that is useful. Their contribution makes them feel valued as individuals, however they need to hold off until they are sure the method works.

Fives are known as investigators because they seek to investigate and understand the most they can about the ways and why things work how they are in nature. They also investigate their own emotions and thoughts. But, they're also one of the toughest skeptical individuals. To try to understand and understand the most they possibly can on the processes of life They challenge the theories of everyone until they're confident in their own beliefs.

The Type Fives having a 4-wing could be considered to be eccentric, whereas the type Fives with Six wings are problem solvers.

Stress Point

When stressed Type Fives they can display unhealthy or negative levels of development that are typically observed among Type Seven personalities.

The unhealthy traits are:

Bipolar

Unpredictable mood changes

Impulsive

Insisting

Unblocked

Adventuresome

Security Point

In times of growth, Type Fives might show healthful or positive levels of development , which are typically found when they are Type Eight personalities.

These traits are healthy and include:

Self-restrained

The most generous

The Resourceful

Decisive

Authoritative

Self-confident

Self-sufficient

Developmental Levels

Healthy:

Level 1

Visionary

Fives with an open mind can create breakthrough discoveries. Their capacity to discover new information is endless.

Level 2

Observationist

They are aware and focussed. Their curiosity draws them to further knowledge.

Level 3

Knowledge Master

They are able to study their chosen subject until they are "master of their field."

Average:

Level 4

Studious

They are obsessed with ensuring that all their theories are correct and work. Blueprints and models are everywhere in their offices.

Level 5

Detached

They are engrossed in offbeat subjects that don't relate to the world of work.

Level 6

Antagonistic

Fives are abrasive and cynical towards anyone who doesn't believe in their beliefs.

Unhealthy:

7th Level

The reclusive

They fear the agression and of the rejection of their opinions, which is why they withdraw from social interactions.

Level 8

Phobic

They are obsessed with the dangers that exist in the world and develop bizarre fear of the world. If they have a one out of a million chances of being exposed to danger, they'll be afraid of it.

Level 9

Schizophrenic

In this moment Fives have suffered an unimaginable break from reality. They are enthralled by their fantasies, and detest the truth.

Chapter 8: Enneagram Personality Type 4 The Artist

Also known as also known as the Individualist or Romantic The artist is driven by the desire to be different. The person wants to feel special and unique and is always searching for their identity. They are seeking to define their self to make them appear different to other people and consequently tend to be self-conscious. They usually view their differences from other people as an advantage or a curse as they are able to clearly set themselves apart from the rest of the crowd. They consider this distinction to be an advantage when it allows them to stay out of the same category as other people. They view it as an obstacle in the sense that it separates them from the peace, tranquility and joy.

What makes an artist a Super Personality? The Artist is very expressive. Since these kinds of people want to be unique in their own way and their lives they tend to be very expressive and pursue creative professions like writing, painting, or other art forms.

The Artist is aware of their own self. The primary goal of an Artist is to discover themselves and what they are worth within the present. They are looking to establish their own identity and strive to achieve this. This is why these types of personalities are often surrounded by beautiful things to induce moods and feelings that show the individuality of their character. Type 4s are also able to recognize and accept their personal emotions and don't try to hide their feelings. They're not afraid of recognizing their own flaws and imperfections.

The Artist is an individual. Due to the honesty of their reflections, artists tend to stay true to their own values and have a strong feeling of being unique. Typ 4s tend to be sensitive people and are often focused on self-expression and self-revelation. They typically express this with their idiosyncratic choices in the way they dress as well as their general appearance.

A Deadly Sin of an Artist

The artist is often misunderstood. The person who is looking for the depth of their relationships and is not able to tolerate superficial encounters and feelings. Because of the unique characteristics they have, Artists frequently believe that they are superior to others, even when they feel an intense desire and envy, because they desire to be acknowledged and valued by others. This means that they are often misunderstood and unappreciated by other people. It also creates anxiety about being flawed or deficient because they don't fit in the mold of the average person. The result is that artists are usually moody and isolated from the rest of society. People often view them as unstable. This is due to the fact that they're often dwelling in their own personal world, where they are constantly analyzing their emotions. Type 4s are often troubled with being present and may get lost in a sense of nostalgia.

The artist is often afflicted with mental illness. Because of their general sadness, the type 4s tend to fall into depression quite easily. They are prone to becoming emotionally and mentally disbalanced due to their self-absorbed nature.

The Artist is typically self-indulgent. They can indulge themselves quickly and then justify it as a means of compensating to make up for their lack of enjoyment in their lives overall. Type 4s are more likely to dreaming up fantasies to ease the stress rather than looking for solutions that can be implemented to fix the issues that make them unhappy.

The artist is usually emotionally detached. Because they tend to get trapped in their own heads Type 4s frequently miss the excitement of being part of a particular circumstance or moment. They are often left with a strong feeling of discontent when their the reality of life doesn't live up the expectations they have inside their heads. They tend to be easily swept off by their own feelings and tend to be more comfortable in the dark emotional realm instead of the bright and happy side.

What Artists Say About Other Personality Types

Artists and. Type 1s

Check out Chapter 2 on how Reformers relate to other types of personality The Reformers and. Type 4s.

Artists and. Type 2s

See Chapter 3 What Helpers Have to Do with Other personality types Helpers and. Type 4s.

Artists against. Type 3s

Check out Chapter 4 on how performers relate to Other personality types The Performers and. Type 4s.

Artists against. Type 5s

The two personalities are very private, and even though they may have different desires, they are able to admire and respect their mutual commitment and intensity to their values and emotions. Most of the time both of these personality types like each other and are considerate of their individual peculiarities. They motivate each one another to be more imaginative. Conflict can arise due to the fact that the artist tends to be more emotionally driven and may require greater intimacy and closeness than Type 5s. Type 5s are more likely to steer aside emotional connection due to the fact that they are thought-provoking and tend to prefer space within their relationships.

Artists against. Type 6s
These two types of personalities are naturally drawn to one the other due to their being emotionally sensitive and are unsure with other people. They're both extremely in tune and are often misinterpreted as one the other. If they are both working on emotional issues, a fusion between these two personalities can result in steadfast determination and practicality. Problems could arise due to the same reason they both are drawn to one in their emotional nature. Both of them are extremely emotional and are prone to feeling overwhelmed. They often challenge each other's loyalty, and then quickly feel a sense of loss. Both types of personalities tend to make self-fulfilling

prophecies out of their reactions and fears towards their relationship.

Artists against. Type 7s

When the two personality types are in a relationship it's the result of opposites drawing. Type 4s are self-doubting, emotional quiet, introverted and type 7s are open, confident, extroverting and optimistic. Type 7s are able to help the Artist overcome shyness issues and a fear of trying new things, or let go of their emotions as the Artist can aid the Enthusiast keep their focus on the things they really would like to achieve. The two types of personality have different ways of thinking and reactivity, but their differences can enable them to enjoy one another. Also, there are issues that could be caused by their different personalities because they both are indecisive and can easily become frustrated with other people when they feel they've been disappointed.

Artists against. Type 8s

Although the artist is emotionally dominant, and the type 8 socially dominant, both can bring passion and fire to a relationship due to the fact that they're both highly sensitive, self-aware and well-informed about what they feel. They are both extremely personalities and may match one another. Because both types are sensitive, their relationship could be unstable in a negative manner when they are rage-ridden as well as depression, anger, and vengeance. They are more prone to disagreements and fights, rather than dealing with conflict with calm heads.

Artists and. Type 9s

Both are shy, private emotional sensitive. They all seek a profound bond with a person and can therefore be an incredibly supportive couple to one the other. Both are naturally sexual and appreciate the ease of being able to be so intimate with another. There are issues that can occur in the event that these two types respond differently to stressful situations. Type 4s are prone to becoming emotional volatile, while Type 9s can become more withdrawn. This can make it difficult to resolve conflicts in relationships, which can lead to its degrading.

What Artists Can Do to Make a Difference in his or her life

The person in question needs to be less shaky in their present and become more attune to their bodies , and less so with their emotions. They must create a more holistic self and master the control of their emotions instead of being lost in them. The practice of heart and root chakra meditation helps them stay grounded and more compassionate toward them and others. Additionally, they could take up navel chakra meditation to boost confidence in themselves and assertiveness. Navel chakra meditation begins by placing your hands in front of your stomach, right below the solar plexus. All fingers must connect at the points. The thumbs should be crossed and your hands straight. While you chant, focus on the navel chakra, which is located in the spine, just above the navel.

Acupressure can also be beneficial. Along with stimulating the points of SP-6 and

LIV-3 LI-4, it can also be stimulated to release the burden of sadness, while the stimulation of LU-1 permits to connect with one's own inner worth. L1-4 is located on the upper side of the hand, between the index finger and the thumb which are joined by the web of flesh. The LU-1 can be found in the chest area just beneath the shoulder.

Other solutions practical that the artist can employ to improve the quality of his or her life are:

* Don't put too much importance on how people are feeling.
* Recognizing that their emotions at the moment are restricted to that particular moment and might not be more significant than the moment itself.

Avoid long conversations that use their minds, particularly when the conversations are overwhelmingly negative or negative.

Do not put things off until you are in the right mindset.

* Committing to be productive and consistently working within"the "real life."

- Engaging in activities that build confidence in their self-esteem and self-confidence.

* committing to regular sleep hours and exercising to increase their outlook and positivity on life.

Practice self-control and avoid actions that could negatively impact their lives like excessive sexual encounters, drug use or alcohol, as well as sleep.

Chapter 9: 10 Specific Steps to Transform Your Life

After you've gained an understanding of yourself and your personal style It's time to apply it to your advantage. You'll need a plan to improve your life, and ultimately reach your goals. This is a complete guideline of the steps to follow to achieve your objectives.

Take the time to embark on this journey

The willingness to change is an obvious thing to do, but most of us don't think how to prepare our minds before. Self-discovery isn't easy therefore you should be ready and willing to dig deeper, perhaps even accepting facts about yourself that aren't happy with since you are aware that it's to serve a higher purpose.

Establishing your goals

Understanding what you are looking for and the reason you're experiencing this personal change is an essential step. Your path may alter throughout the process, therefore you must ensure that your goals for yourself are achievable and achievable. For instance, I wanted to be a more confident and secure person. And in my mind as I was figuring out my personality traits and particular traits, I always had this goal in my mind.

Understanding your personality kind

Learn what the personality is and learn about the traits it. Through taking any of these personality test we discussed in the past, you'll be able to better understand your personality characteristics. It is important to learn about your personality and how you relate your personality to the way you've lived your life up to now. It is possible to detect several different personality types that are in your personality, which is extremely typical. It's not possible to be only one "Challenger" or be a 100 "Loyalist." It is the Ennagram can be extremely helpful to understand the personality qualities and flaws you have and to build upon that.

Making the necessary changes

While it may not be an easy task when you analyze your personality and understanding your strengths, you will be able to pinpoint areas you're required to make improvements, or alter your habits or thoughts. If you are an extrovert, introvert, or cautious, you'll modify the traits you wish to improve to change each day at one time. Perhaps you are required to have a new relationship, or be more attractive, or you just need to understand the character of others in order to better communicate and be more comfortable. The most important thing to be successful is to accept the changes you're putting in place. If you're resistant then you are the only one who stands on the way to your personal change.

Learn from your mistakes

Since you are trying to transform something that's likely to be deeply rooted in you, for example, your lack of trust or to be naive, anticipate that it will be a long and difficult process that will be filled with challenges. If you fall and fall, don't get angry and instead, be grateful that you have been provided with an opportunity to grow. If you've always been one who thinks about other people and never think about yourself, you'll struggle to change your behavior for the better. You might say yes to a request, but really mean not, and that's acceptable. But, you'll be able to recall the next time you felt when you gave to the temptation and then not standing your rights You will then rectify the situation following time. You will be able to say no and become happy with it.

The right attitude to adopt

Positive thinking is key for success. You must always to believe in the plan you're putting into practice If you don't you believe in it, who would? There are a variety of ways to cultivate a positive mindset and meditation is a way to break off and concentrate your thoughts on what you're trying to achieve. Through refocusing and having an uncluttered mind, you are able to do whatever it is you're trying to accomplish more effectively. In addition, repetition of positive affirmations can make a difference when experiencing any kind of change. For instance, on the journey to work or meet with someone, tell yourself how much strength or confidence you possess in case you are working to improve your confidence.

Re-evaluating your dreams and goals

Recommit. Once you've determined what aspects of your personality that you don't like or want to be different, you'll likely have to change the direction of your life across a variety of sectors and areas. Take a moment to record your new objectives and then evaluate them in the long and short-term. Perhaps, for instance, you recognize that leader talent within you but , in the past you've always been afraid of failing. After you've mastered the art of to balance your personality and abilities, you should definitely begin contemplating the possibility of starting your own business. You can do it!

Get the necessary support

Don't be afraid to include other people in the process. For instance, if you're married and stable Your new goals will definitely affect on your wife, and you should make sure you get them up to level. They could be your ally, and ought to be. Your partnership should improve each of you lives. You may also solicit assistance from other people in your professional or spiritual life. Do not be afraid to explain the goals to children about what you're trying to achieve, since they will be taught valuable life lessons. They can also be your greatest supporter while you work to change certain behaviors and how you react to others. Be sure to surround your self with the appropriate people in order to achieve your goals.

Accepting yourself completely

In the final phase of this process or journey you will be able to discover the most important knowledge of all that is love and acceptance of yourself. When you are aware of who you are, and then changing your actions based on situation and the circumstances this is a good thing. Your environment may also be the reason why you need to be changed or adapted and you should consider this possibility, too.

Rewards yourself

It's important to acknowledge and celebrate your accomplishments. If you've reached the goal you set for yourself, or you've been able to move forward in your personal journey, congratulate your self on the back. It will motivate you to keep going and will often help you look at what's been successful, and you will be able to duplicate it the next time.

Chapter 10: The Enneagram Types of Personality Myths & The Facts

To maximize the benefits of understanding what is your Enneagram personal type, it is important to need to put aside the commonly held beliefs that circulate. The fact that these myths exist is similar to the dearth of accurate information. When you cannot find reliable and reliable sources, those that you find are legitimate. But the belief in these myths make it difficult to comprehend Enneagram as well as yourself as well as other people. The primary goal for this article is to concentrate on the most commonly-held beliefs and the (in)accuracy.

The Enneagram tests do not really work, and they're not reliable.

The idea of Enneagram personality tests aren't effective originates from disagreement with your character. If you don't agree with something does not mean that it's wrong. The goal of the Enneagram test is not to determine positive or negative personality types however, it is to highlight your strengths, traits, and weaknesses to enhance your self-discovery and understanding about the world. To get the most accurate results, adhere to the suggestions that is provided in the earlier chapters of the book (sign up for a seminar and seek out guidance from someone with expertise, or do it on the internet). If you're on the internet, the most reliable tests aren't always cost-free, however you shouldn't throw them away as soon as you can, since there's no way you'll be using the same thing daily.

The personality type of your character is easy to identify when you're young.

It's not entirely true and the reason is straightforward the fact that your personality is fluid when you are younger then 21 to 22. While you might are a dominant type of personality and might exhibit traits that are that are shared by others occasionally It's much easier to identify your personality type when you're in the middle or late-twenties than later during your lifetime. Do not be too focused on your age to determine whether you're young or old to recognize your personality kind. What is most important is to know your inner patterns of thinking, behavior or feeling, and then take the test honestly.

Sixes are often misidentified as Fours are often misinterpreted as. Therefore, if your persona is Four, that means that you're actually Six.

The personality kinds Six and Four share several similarities and it's not unusual for people to confuse them as each other. Actually, the odds are greater that people will think you're Six (if you're Four) rather than are doing it yourself. While both personality types have a lot in common but they also have significant distinctions. The important thing to remember is to not think "well this personality type is also applicable to me, therefore it is the case" and recognize your preferred kind of personality.

You can determine a person's personality type from the manner in which they conduct themselves during arguments.

A person's personality type can have an impact on how they behave in various situations, including disputes, but it's the most accurate way to tell the type of person they are. Different people view certain circumstances differently, which is why it's difficult to determine a person's personality kind during a debate in the absence of knowing their behavior habits. Additionally, different people behave in different situations of argument. For instance, you may not behave the same way when having a heated debate on the internet and at work.

Ones are rigid, neat freaks.

If you've studied the Enneagram in the past, you've probably encountered theories on the different personality types. The most popular belief is that the Type One is a perfect freak and a rigid person due to their obsession with perfection. Of course, you'll meet Ones who fit this description, but that does not mean that all are. It's all about the individual's beliefs about the right or wrong , and their ideal method to accomplish something. So, if someone believe that flexibility can be essential to solve a particular issue and they believe that flexibility is the answer, then they'll do.

Twos are extremely dependent.

The person that is diagnosed as Type 2 generally viewed as being in need because of their generosity which can cause them to forget their own requirements. They want to stand out as irreplaceable. However, these do not suggest that someone is excessively dependent. Always consider the positive and applaud their generosity.

Threes are focused on themselves and their own ambitions.

Although everyone Performer would like to accomplish the goals that he or she has set for themselves however, that doesn't mean that they don't care about the other people around them. Indeed their positive outlook can serve as motivation for others, so that they can achieve their goals as well.

Your most enjoyable and satisfying way

We mentioned it at the start of our journey towards discovering and understanding the Enneagram This system of typing is based upon an ancient method developed over time to assist us in applying it more effectively.

The current Enneagram is divided into nine points and divided into three triads, or centers. These triads are the brain, heart and the gut, which are called the center of thinking, the center of sensation and the heart of the instincts. They are the fundamental elements of the human psyche.

There are a myriad of systems for determining personality types but the Enneagram is distinct from the crowd , and is the reason why it maintains its worldwide repute. In addition to dipping deeper into the variety occur even within your preferred type, but it also gives an unique element to the process.

Namely:

The direction you're given is integration, which is a description of the way your type will perform on a health and growth path. Additionally, you're provided with an indication of the disintegration direction which explains how your kind will behave under stress and pressure.

The process of self-discovery is more extensive than the typical personality typing systems since it grants you the ability to analyze and make conscious choices in every aspect that you are in, not just relationships. If you're looking to take their own personal development and self-awareness to a higher stage, this is an essential instrument.

The Enneagram is a diagnostic tool to help you understand the personality (ego) and the way it functions. It is about being aware of who truly are, the core habits that guide your behavior and the character you can develop to build a progress in your life or a degrading path is the start of your self-discovery.

Based on your nature, there will be certain passions that you should be aware of and strive to transform at the underlying level. When you take a closer look at your actions and motivations and motives, the easier to transform them into positive virtues since as you will recall at when the novel was first published we declared that each one individual is pure, and good at heart.

Chapter 11: A Persona Road Map Test

"Enneagram is among the most effective and insightful tools to understand our own and other people. In essence, the Enneagram assists us in seeing our self on a deeper than a more objective perspective and can provide invaluable help in the process of gaining self-knowledge."
- -- the Enneagram Institute.

You want to get to know who you are .Right?

In the absence of controversy, personal identity is among the most important aspects in life that people are eager to gain knowledge about. Self-knowledge is among the most important aspects that people have been trying to exclaim about. We would like to know more about ourselves, our talents and creative capabilities, our physical health, strengths and weaknesses, strengths the virtues, blind spots and many other aspects.

Rachel Simons said, "Self-knowledge is the key to real success." What is the reason true? When you are aware of yourself that you are able to start the process of bringing out the best you. Oprah declared that the main goal for every person is to be "the most authentic, highest quality version of themselves". One way you can begin realizing your full potential and becoming the best version of yourself is to understand yourself.

It all begins with understanding the person we are today in comparison to the person we'd like to have in the near future. The person you'll be in the near future is the result of the effort you put into yourself now. The more you understand yourself and work on improving yourself more, the greater your chance being the kind of person that you would like to be in the near future.

The Enneagram provides a unique, more profound way to comprehend our own self. As per the Enneagram Institute, "Enneagram is one of the most effective and effective tools to understand us and others." It is at the core it is that the Enneagram assists us in seeing our self on a higher understanding, more objective, and is a valuable aid in our quest to gain self-knowledge."

It's one thing knowing about the Enneagram however it's a totally different matter to utilize the Enneagram to determine your personal traits and use that knowledge to transform into the "highest real and authentic version of you." In regards to the Enneagram there are two major ways to discover your personal type: self-reflection method, and a test-taking technique.

Joe Carter said, "Determining the validity of the Enneagram is a challenge since there is no established test or method to determine the types of personality. The oldest versions that make up Enneagram classification are self-assessment which is where the person selects the type that best matches their personality. Although this can be assisted by a short questionnaire, the method of classification is based mostly on personal experience."

Instead of debating which method is best for you, the best way to understand your own self is to utilize both forms. Take an Enneagram test from a reliable site or Enneagram test provider . Then, be able to say "This myself!" That means self-reflection following the test, and taking the test in conjunction with your own reflection to select the number.

How do I begin with the personality Test and what steps do we Should To

Please, know this: the test for personality test is only for one person. Nobody will take the test for you. It is not possible to have someone person take the test for you and then inform you of your test type. It's an individual thing. It is necessary to take the test on your own If you are interested in knowing your own. This is crucial and should not be undervalued!

It is also important to realize that the principle behind this Enneagram does not intend to place you into a box. You must ensure you understand yourself in a deeper manner. This is among the reasons to consider doing an Enneagram test that will help you identify your wings type and your main kind. Select one Enneagram test that can help you with the knowledge and another aspect of your wing.

There are four primary elements of An Enneagram Test:

The Enneagram personal information: If you're looking for a site that will offer a better Enneagram test, make sure to look over the background information on their site to ensure you understand how they plan and create the Enneagram testing and reporting system. If their typing system for personality isn't accurate it means that the test results you receive is also not accurate. Review all the information they offer about their typing system. It is also possible to be aware of the kinds of tests they provide. There are websites that could offer a comparative test in addition to the typical type of questions that are based on questions. Choose which is the most appropriate for you.

The Enneagram Questionnaire This questionnaire is called the Enneagram is a methodical and systematic personality typing system which helps you find your unique number. The questions you ask will help you determine and locate your number. Answering the questions honestly and accurately can be the best way to determine the most suitable number for you.

It is the score of your Enneagram. This is the fundamental Enneagram Score provides you with an insight into the person you are and what you stand in relation with the Enneagram. You are aware of your fundamental and basic Enneatype. The score is determined by the information you give in your Enneagram test. If you don't know what each personality type means you may not fully know the result.

It is the Enneagram Report: Reading the entire report can help you understand you more. It is essential to gain a comprehensive understanding on what you learn from the Enneagram test, not being a victim of the test and being a victim of your own. You must know how the results are related to and affect your personal growth.

How do you identify the best matches and define the Personality

How do you find the persona that is most compatible with what you're currently doing? What is the best way to choose your type of personality? What do you look for to declare that my enneatype is? There isn't any definitive and absolute rule for this.

Take a look at the whole picture of all the character descriptions.

Before you can take your Enneagram test, it is essential to be able to see a large image of all the Enneagram description types. This will allow you to get a better understanding of the different numbers. The concept behind an Enneagram can be that are all nine types in our bodies. However, depending on our your childhood and experiences throughout life, one type is predominant in our lives.

This type is the one that is the basis of our way of living and our philosophy. In addition there are different types that mix with the fundamental kind of. The basic and wings-type personality can help you gain a better understanding of what you're like. It can help you paint more of a image of your present state.

Take a look at the motives, instead of the behaviors.

Motives drive our actions every day. Remember that it isn't just what someone does, but the reason why they do it. The Enneagram helps to understand the people's emotional needs and how they perform certain behaviors in order to fulfill their emotional needs. This is why the Enneagram an exceptional instrument to understand the person we are.

People's actions are simply the expression of their most profound and most predominant emotional desire. What people do are a reflection of their dominant emotional need and desire. For instance Type Nines are driven by relationships. They want to create relationships, build and maintain them. They don't be irritable or have issues with others. They are therefore comfortable being a bit smug at times in their lives, so long as it's maintaining good relations with other people.

In contrast Type Eights are highly competitive. They are competitive and want to beat the competition. They are determined to conquer other people and businesses. They would like to lead. On the other hand these people might be willing to break relationships in order to ensure they are successful. The people naturally inclined to nine who are adept at hiring and firing others.

However, people who are type 8 love to be at peace. If they're in a position of management the peace-making emotion makes it difficult for them to fire people even when they have to. It can take some time and can be painful to let go of individuals. It could even over the line before they take this decision.

Motivations are crucial. It's not only about the behavior. It's about the way we communicate our deep desire to feel. This is the aspect you should pay attention to when making use of the Enneagram to identify the perfect persona for you. Consider, what emotion do I feel the most often motivated by? It might be worthwhile to take a look at the Enneatypes and determine the motivations/emotional needs which drive the behavior and actions of each type.

Typ 1: The Idealist Idealistic and rational driven type

Type 2: The caring, Giving, Generous and interpersonal driven type

Type 3: The Achievement image, performance, achievement and Outstanding Type that is driven by

Type 4 - Beauty, imaginative, creative and Artistic Type that is driven by

Type 5: The investigative Perception driven, and Knowledge Type

Type 6: The security Loyalty, and Suspicion Driven Type

Type 7 is the enthusiastic, Fun Loving and Spontaneous Busy Type

Typ 8 The Challenge Dominating Competitively, Conquering Type 8 that is driven

Type 9 - Peace, easygoing, mediation, relationship Type that is built driven

Beware of using the Enneagram as a tool to label individuals.

This is the first thing we start to do. When we recognize that we have the Enneagram Then we begin to categorize and classify people based on their possible behaviors or actions. Remember that regardless of what the labels you choose to use they are just assumption.

"Okay I can see how bossy he can be. He is always trying to be in control and manage people's lives. This is why he's an "A Type Eight." Actions and patterns of thought like this one don't help. This Enneagram device isn't designed for disintegration, but rather for bringing together people. It's designed to help you understand you and others in order that you can lead a fulfilling and meaningful life.

The Enneagram tool isn't focused on building walls of bitterness, anger or resentment against people. It is important to use the tool to get to know people and develop an authentic relationship with them instead of simply defining them as one of a specific kind. If a person exhibits characteristics of a certain type and characteristics, you must employ the Enneagram tool to adjust and adapt to create an effective rapport with the person instead of being judgemental and critical.

Chapter 12: Warding Off Yourself From Unwanted emotions

Being an empath it is important to know how to safeguard yourself from unwanted emotions. Perhaps, you've practiced safeguarding and grounding yourself using the techniques you've learned before so you have a basic understanding of the best way to safeguard yourself. You may however believe that these techniques aren't enough, since your energy could be a bit exposed or vulnerable in some situations. Therefore, you'll need to work on your protection capabilities and discover ways to guard yourself from negative energy-related experiences.

In this chapter, we're going to look at ways you can safeguard yourself by developing your own grounding and shielding strategies that will allow you to get protection from negative feelings and energies. So, you'll be able to be confident and take complete control of your energy and experience as you move through your life. This chapter you'll be introduced to a variety of grounding and shielding techniques, and will learn when each technique should be utilized. In the next chapter, you will be guided in creating your own unique grounding and shielding technique which you can use whenever you require an effective anchor to defend you from the elements and those who are around you. It is recommended to keep this book in your pocket in case you need to draw on the other strategies that are taught in this book to help you if you discover that your personal defense method isn't quite sufficient in some situations.

Different types of shields

Empaths can avail quite many different kinds of shields they can use to defend themselves from danger in areas of high-energy or in public spaces. In general there are three types of shields that you may want to use as well as your white energy ball you've already practiced for a while. They include an mirror shield as well as a spike shield and brick shield.

Mirror shields require you to first construct your white ball-shaped energy shield around yourself in order to mentally align up the exterior of the shield with mirrors directed towards the outside. This shield can help send energy back to where it came from. This means that even if someone wants to throw negative energy at you it will be sent back to them via your mirror. So, people like narcissists, for instance, who might try to harm you , are not able to do so because their energy is directed back to them.

A spike shield is which you build the white ball of energy around you , and then imagine it drawing large spikes towards you, and huge spikes out to the universe. It blurs the boundaries of your shield and allows the user to "mix" and blend with energy around you without actually allowing it be absorbed directly into your personal energy field. This is a fantastic shield to have for when you want to blend better into the environment when you are in busy public areas.

Brick shields are constructed in the same manner, beginning with the white energy ball the final stage is to imagine the entire exterior of your shield covered with bricks. Imagine that you are building a brick wall around you, keeping yourself in a safe place. These shields can be extreme, so it is best to stay away from using them unless you're likely to be in a dangerous and energetic environment like one that has an ego-centric person. This way, none of their energy is able to penetrate your space and you'll be safe and free from their destructive energy field.

Techniques to Ground Yourself

As with the shielding technique, there's numerous ways to be grounded and remain safe from energies which may inadvertently enter your private space. Sometimes, shields may contain energy leaks, or the pressure of keeping other people's energy out can cause an intense energy build up within of your personal energy field. This can cause exhaustion and prevent you from having a clear, comfortable and energizing energy field which can cause you to feel weighed down, creating the burdensome experience as an empath.

When it comes to establishing a solid foundation there are three methods that you can practice along with picturing roots growing from your tailbone, or your feet, and reaching into the earth below. One of them involves the earth and the other two are based on water, that, as you've probably guessed is essential to help you deal with emotions efficiently.

The earth connection is sometimes referred to "earthing" and requires you to walk in the open air for a short period of time. It is recommended that you are walking on soil or grass since they are considered to be the most pure kind of earth energy, connecting you to the earth beneath. While walking on the ground, it is believed that the earth pulls unwanted energy from your body via the soles of your feet . It also assists you in maintaining an energy field that is clean.

Another method you could try is taking Epsom baths that contain salt to purify your energy. Water is famous for its cleansing properties as well as salt has been believed to help ward away negative energies that could remain within your energy field, making you feel heavy and exhausted. When you soak in the Epsom salt bath lasting at least 30 mins it will help you release undesirable negative emotions, and feel light and rejuvenated.

If you don't like baths, then you might prefer this third option which is cleansing showers. Cleansing showers can be utilized together with a visual practice to cleanse yourself of any negative energies. To do this, take a shower and imagine the water taking away any negative energy or feelings that appear to be stuck within the energy fields of your. If you'd like to it, close your eyes and imagine the water rushing away from you like it was becoming black due to negativity and keep imagining it until it becomes clear. The visualisation of the water changing to clear indicates that the negative energy is gone and that you have been cleared and grounded from any negative emotional and physical energies.

Creating Your Unique Protection Formula

In the same way as all other ways of dealing with your empathic nature and defending yourself from external influences it is likely that you will need to create your own personal formula for protection to ensure that you are free from negative emotions. The best method to develop your personal formula is to begin using the mentioned shields and grounding techniques , and then discover what works for your personal needs.

Here are three steps that can assist you to create your own personal protection formula, so you are completely secure and secure at all times.

Step 1: Practice all methods

Doing your best to practice all the shields of protection and grounding techniques included in this book are will provide you with the perfect chance to test the various shields and feel how it will help you when in use. Every person is drawn to different strategies and discover that different methods are more effective for them or blend more easily into their daily routine Therefore, don't be uneasy to try different strategies and find what is most compatible for your personal needs. It is possible to record any experiences that you experience in your journal to be able to recall the way each shield or grounding method helped you, and the one that made you feel the most comfortable after. It is recommended to try the strategies 3 times at a minimum in order that you get the full picture of the way it feels like. In the absence of this, you might be unable to benefit from it as much since it takes time to get the technique to use and then grow from it.

Step 2: Assess Your Unique Circumstances

After you've practiced making your own shields and grounding techniques It is important to ensure that you are developing a unique protection strategy that will work for the majority of your daily life events. If you are constantly pulled into busy environments and feel vulnerable and exposed you could benefit the most from a spike-based shield. If you're constantly vulnerable to narcissists and energy parasites, you could be able to benefit by a mirror shield, with some bricks. If you're not located near nature, you might be more benefited from taking baths or showers that are grounded. Find methods that will be suited to your specific life and preferences and begin applying them on a regular basis to ensure that you can build on techniques that are actually beneficial to you. Rememberthat the more time you spend practicing an activity, the more efficient and more efficient it'll be since your brain and your energy get more accustomed to this routine. This means that as soon as you begin your practice, you'll begin to feel better since it is used often in your daily everyday life. This is the reason why you should have an "signature" way of life is essential as consistency is the only way to build protection from unwanted emotions and energies.

Step 3: Customize Based on your intuition

While you're going through the process you will feel asked to modify your grounding and protection methods to allow you to experience complete freedom from any unwanted emotional or physical energy. Maybe, you're inspired to put a mirror on your spikes or are looking to shower and apply the soap bar that has Himalayan pink salt. You might even be feeling a need to meditate and lay down next to living plants, or doing something in order to safeguard yourself that your inner voice is calling you to. Take this intuition into consideration and follow it with your actions, because your senses will guide to the path you should follow in order to protect yourself. Trust your instincts.

Your Quick Start Action Step: Secure and ground

The first step to take this morning is to practice each of the shields described in the chapter. By doing this you will begin to get a sense of what each shield is like and how it will serve the best. Concentrate on the one most likely to assist you the most in your situation and commitment to using it for at least three times in the following day or two whenever you feel you have to. So, you can begin to practice creating your own special shield and put it to use. If you are in a sense prompted to create an additional step, personalize it in one way or other, or try something completely different, don't hesitate to listen to your intuition. This will help you build a stronger defense and is definitely worth the efforts and time.

Chapter 13: Enneagram as A Universal symbol of an ancient teaching

Human beings are characterized by three primary methods of experiencing the world. This could be through thought or feeling, as well as sensation. The Enneagram model, along with other spiritual theories consider three intelligence centers and perception. These influence the experiences individuals experience and their responses to them. These correspond to the head, heart and body. As a psychologist's point standpoint, everyone uses all three of them. Everyone is aware of the world around them and experiences an emotional reaction to it. They also think about the world around them, but each could choose one as the primary channel for the perception and reaction to incidents. Each of the centers has its own method of living and its own negative emotions and worries which are connected. The most prevalent types in each triad are ones that are favorable to the specific center and offer methods for managing the issue.

Given the many sets of three that comprise the Enneagram of Personality There are a variety of ways to break down the entire Enneagram in bite-sized pieces of three. It could take a while to process the vast amount of information and it is possible that you will not be able to have it all incorporated in the first attempt. If you are using the Enneagram to serve the purpose of being a number, and to give up and justify mistakes, then that is not the right way to go. The purpose is to make use of the Enneagram as a platform to discover yourself and grow personally. After years of research and observation the Enneagram will allow you to reveal your true self and reveal your secrets.

The Body Center

The body center is the intelligence of the body, which is an experience that is direct and immediate of our lives as well as having alive as well as connecting with yourself and being in contact and other elements. If you're not in the present it is difficult to feel a feeling of self-confidence, being and completeness. The primary emotion of the body's core is anger. This is typically an instinctual reaction to the feeling of being in conflict or being in danger of being mishandled. The subconscious fear is about unity, and that is the reason people can become lost and their function or stop functioning properly. The body's center requires autonomy and is worried about its influence on the environment.

In this way an individual who is a Type Eight may tend to display their anger quite easily or quickly. They might also put their guards up quickly so that no one is able to be able to touch them or hurt their feelings. Their anger could stem from many different situations in which they or a person suffers inequity.

The Head Center

It is here that the thinking happens and also reflection, analysis and projection of thoughts about the way that other people or events should be. The types that are based on the head include the 5, 6, and 7 and may react to their surroundings with the help of their thoughts. They also may have vivid imaginations and is a great capacity to analyze and connect thoughts. Some people who are social claim to be content with the company created by their own ideas. For these types, thinking is a means of prevention of anxiety.

The mind needs to maintain all its defenses in place and develop an unconnected sense of self and create a sense of direction. The primary emotion that is about the head center is anxiety. When you sense the presence and the stillness in a clear way you can experience it as the foundation of all things. This is the source of faith. When you fall off the foundation of guidance and support You may feel panicky and scared. The type with the head center requires security and is concerned with the beliefs they hold and their strategy. The Type Five might be averse to fear by recoiling in their minds and reducing their personal requirements. There is a need , for instance, to be able to master something to feel secure and look around to evaluate what's happening. The Type Sixes are able to respond to fear by contemplating what could occur in the worst case scenario. The Type Sevens react to fear by trying to change uncomfortable, uncomfortable or stressful situations into something that is exciting and fresh to prevent anxiety. They may be scared of being in grief, pain, or fear and engage in activities that help them escape or keeps them engaged.

The Heart Center

It is in this place that people experience emotions , or sensations that inform people of how they feel and not what they believe about something. Heartfelt emotions can be anything from dramatic and unjust up to subtle or indifferent emotions. The majority of people feel connected to others within this group, however they are seeking satisfaction and affection. These are the three types of people, 2, and 4. They have distorted perceptions of their emotions. The heart is conscious of the truth, and lets us know the truth about identity, as well as the reality of our identity. It is also the place where people get a sense of the significance and glory of their lives. If someone says something that resonates and is authentic, your heart will feel in agreement and you may feel connected to the message as well as towards the subject. In this way, being connected to the heart is a sign of the quality of being and shows how to discern the truth. Another typical emotion associated with the heart's centre is shame. The kinds 2, 3 and 4 are searching for validation, recognition and mirroring. This is necessary because , when you're young, you have only a small capacity for self-reflection. You only know who you are from other people's perspectives. Therefore, if you are not getting the attention you'd want, you feel a sense of guilt, deficiency and feeling of emptyness. The head centers demand lots of attention and are concerned about how they are perceived or the image they project of themselves.

The Type Twos may be caring for others to build rapport with others and to not feel shameful. They could make a person appear loved or appreciated even but they aren't sure what they require or feel. They usually realize this since they have many people who depend on them for their survival. The Type Threes are disconnected from their inner being and believe they require positive feedback and praise from others. They can discover the value and self-worth they deserve through their work to prevent feelings of shame that can result. They also attempt to project positive images into the world and seek the praise of others to boost their self-esteem.

The Type Fours typically search for reasons that they are different with other people. They create and maintain moods, and utilize emotions as a method by which they are able to protect themselves from being dismissed. They do this by exaggeration of their grievances and losses, which causes them to suppress their feelings and to attract attention or pity from people. In this way, the Type Twos project shame and construct images of themselves as a successful person They feel uncomfortable because they feel many shames and hide this by creating the image of their success. The Type Fours can hide their shame and have created an image that reflects their individuality.

How do the Enneagram Centers Work

There is a lot to be discussed about the way personality evolves within the Enneagram. Every type has its own center even though everyone is a part of and is affected by head, heart and bodies centers within them in various ways. The Enneagram describes the different characteristics of the center for all human beings it is a system that is universal to all and illustrating how it manifests in different ways depending on the various types.

It is true that we have "two two of us" within us all, which is the true self-known, and the self-perceived personality who is convinced that it is the true self of an person. Between the two the personality tends to show itself through routine narrow-minded thinking patterns and survival responses. They are known as fixation, passion and instinctual subtypes. They can be the cause of repetitiveness throughout our lives. The concept of the primary self, the heart and the head permits the holy opposite, which is an individual feature of the nature. They are also known as holy virtues and the holy idea. The concept of virtue and the holy concept are more similar to holy seeds than to holy opposites because they are all present when they are born and identify the qualities that are divine to the soul. The people have forgotten this when they became accustomed to the world and created the personality defense systems. The personality conceals and shields the core self, and it is also a mirror that acts as mirrors that reflect the front and back while looking for the forgotten parts in the external world rather than the inside. This is the root of the distinctions between the nine kinds. In short, one of the basic structures that define the different types is that they each have different ways of manifesting. For each of them types, their spirituality and their psychological self appear to focus on the goal of trying to replicate the natural undiscovered qualities of their particular type.

The Head Center is a Holy Idea

The focus is an indicator of the person's usual preoccupation or the center of their focus. It could be described as a imaginary hamster on the wheel of mental thought. The holy concept however is a state of awareness that is felt rather than being thought of by the spiritual center in the moment it is not a fixed thought.

The Heart Center: Passion and Holy Virtue

The typical underlying emotion of the heart is referred to as Passion. The early Christians were aware of this as one of the nine obstacles to the life of prayer as described by the philosopher Evagrius Ponticus. Presently, they relate to the seven sins that are deadly which are in addition to deceit and fear. The state of being felt within the heart is referred to as

Holy Virtue. It's also called the virtue of being in the heart.

The Body Center

Subtypes are three survival instincts that are linked to the center of the body that is the Enneagram. Survival is the issue between life and death is viewed as the final decision by unconscious gut reactions and instinct. The nine passions and fixations determine the traits of the persona and are recognizable as "what one performs." These subtypes provide three distinct ways of expressing each one, causing the actions of these types to be interpreted as being a matter of life or death.

These instincts are based on the vitality of a particular area like:

Self-preservation is the only way to live with the passion that is focused on the material wellbeing.

It is also a sociological aspect of belonging as humans are tribal members. The survival of a tribe is contingent on the tribe's acceptance.

Sexual needs exist because everyone has the right to love. It is also linked to the desire to endure in the new world developed in one-on-one relationships, regardless of whether it is a baby or a validation by a different person.

Every person tends to concentrate on one or the other dependent on their experiences in the face of the biggest danger to their core when they were growing up. It is also a matter of whether the children had food and shelter, felt loved, well-cared for and accepted by their family and their efforts to find unconditional love. In the present, there is a controversy over whether the subtype is present since the moment of birth, regardless of whether it's due to developmental factors and the environment or some combination of both exactly the same way as the person's adult self is. The outcome is that while all three of them are essential for living a fulfilled life, only one is likely to be viewed in a way that is not conscious as the primary source of danger or pain. This is why it brings lots of energy in the form of attention and energy. It appears as one of the best sources of satisfaction and happiness.

Chapter 14: The Theory Of Enneagram

There is no way to be 100% sure of the exact location where the Enneagram theory originated. Many believe that it is rooted to mathematics, while others say that it was a result of religious beliefs and Christianity. Plotinus is an ancient Greek philosopher, who was born around 200 A.D was a proponent of nine tenets of the human persona. Ramon Llull, a mathematician in the 13th century, also discussed nine personality types (Cloete, n.d.).

But, regardless of how long you go back to trace the Enneagram theory there is an evolution in the theory. The Enneagram theories is an image, that is used to help identify the person's personality. But, psychologists have also employed this theory to recognize people who are in larger crowds (Cloete, n.d.).

How it Does It Work

One of the most distinctive aspects concerning this Enneagram theory is that it doesn't place people in an order. Within the nine primary types of personality, there exist 27 different subtypes. In addition for each person, there are lines, wings as well as other aspects which determine your individual persona (Cloete, n.d.). While the concept and diagram may appear complicated at first, because it's complex it becomes simpler to comprehend when you understand the specifics about the subtypes, types, and how the theory operates generally.

Diagrams

To help you comprehend the diagram of the Enneagram You will need to study the diagram step-by-step. This will help you comprehend and follow the fundamental outline that is the Enneagram. For example, you could begin by examining the diagram as an arc. In this circle, you'll be able to see the numbers 9 through one. Although the numbers are numerals, if you move counterclockwise, they're ordered in a sequential order and that's why nine is on top. Each of the nine numbers is a type of personality and can be identified in the above diagram.

Many people are confused by the lines that make up the circle. As you can observe, there are a variety of lines that run through the numbers from one to another. These lines lead you to your personal identity and to the wings of your personality. Also, if you study the lines in a sequential fashion you'll gain an comprehension of Enneagram.

Then, look at the numbers nine three, six, and nine. If they're connected to form an Equilateral triangle. From there, you'll need to consider the connections of numbers between six points, which form an irregular hexagon. You should be sure to adhere to the following order since the points must be arranged in this order.

Number 1 is connected to number number 4.

Number 4 is connected to number 2 and connects to

Number 2 is connected to number 8.

Number 8 is connected to number number 5 and connects to
Number 5 is connected to number 7
number 7 connects to number 1

When you examine the lines of the Enneagram you will notice the presence of arrows that will lead you to the next number.

9 Types and 27 Subtypes

It is not a good idea to think that your personality will fall under only one category of personality. Actually, you'll see a few aspects of your personality that are shared by every personality. But, it is important to discover the main number that is in your personal profile. The number you choose will be the largest portion in your persona. Keep in mind that the Enneagram is designed to get you out of a mold rather than place you in one. That's why your character is scattered across the diagram, however there will be one central number.

Within this segment, I'll look at the different types and subtypes which can make up your character. I will not discuss these subtypes and types in depth within this section.

The nine personality kinds in the Enneagram are as follows (Berkers, n.d.):

The Perfectionist

The Helper

The Achiever

The Individualist

The Investigator

The Loyalist

The Enthusiast

The Protector

The Mediator

There are 27 subtypes in the nine types of personality. Three categories are the main ones that contain these subtypes. They include self-preservation, social as well as one-on-one (Cloete, n.d.).

The social section concentrates on how we interact with others and our social skills. It defines how we manage our connections and the way we interact with other people. Social categories also focus on the way we try to do our best can for our fellow human beings (Cloete, n.d.).

Self-preservation is a term that refers to the way we protect our bodies and minds. It's about how we handle stress and other life-related circumstances. The focus is on our feelings. This category examines ways to be the best we can in order to protect our physical, mentally and physically (Cloete, n.d.).

The one-on one category focuses on the legacy we wish to leave for the next generation. Every person, within your own family or the world, would like to be remembered once they pass away. This topic examines how we can manage these kinds of circumstances. It also focuses on the more intimate relationships we have with other people and the environment. With this type of analysis it is possible to decide the things we would like to leave to the next generation and how we would like to be the best we can while on this planet (Cloete, n.d.).

Every personality type has a subtype in the self-preservation and social and one-on one category. To get a better understanding of this, because it's a bit complicated I'll list every personality type along with its classification and its subtypes below. I will explore the subtypes in more detail later.

The Perfectionist
Social: Unadaptable
Self-preservation Do not worry
One-on-one: Zeal

The Helper
Social Ambition
Self-preservation: Privilege
One-on-one Seduction

The Achiever
Social: Prestige
Self-defense: Security
One-on-one: Charisma

The Individualist
Social Themes: Shame
Self-preservation: Tenacity
One-on-one: Competitors

The Investigator
Social Totem
Self-protection: Castle
One-on-one: Secure

The Loyalist
Social Duty

Self-preservation Warmth
One-on-one: Fear of being intimidated
The Enthusiast
Social Sacrifice
Self-preservation: Network
One-on-one: Fascination
The Protector
Social: Solidarity
Self-preservation The goal is satisfaction
One-on-one Possession
The Mediator
Social: Participation
Self-protection: Appetite
One-on-one: Fusion
Center Points
Beyond the lines and numbers Beyond the lines and numbers, the diagram is broken down into 3 triads or a central point which include the head, heart and body. These centers further enhance your character by describing your most frequently used emotions.

1. Heart Center

The heart's central point is the numbers of four, three and two. Since the heart is believed to be the leader of emotion and truth The numbers indicate those who are typically more sensitive and believes that we must be authentic about who we really are. People who are in the center of their heart feel a deep sense of being connected to truth.

The most frequent emotion that comes to the heart's center is shame. They are extremely concerned about their appearance and the way others perceive their image. They don't feel satisfied with themselves until they are in a position to see their self through the eyes of another.

As with the other center, the heart is not without weaknesses and strengths However, the strengths and weaknesses of this center are determined by the personality type you possess. For instance, the Type four's strengths are different from the type two's ("Heart Triad" n.d.).

Wing Points

The wing points represent the aspects of your personality which are distributed to the two types of personality that are adjacent to you (Cloete, n.d.). While these two personality types aren't as extensive as your main personality They are significant since they can balance your personality. For example, if you are an 'point four' personality type the next type could be an 'A. The other types can be considered to be in contradiction to one's personality, however they are crucial, to fully comprehend the entirety of a person's personality. This is the reason why there are theories and tests such as the Enneagram. It not only allows us to learn about us better, but it helps other people such as psychologists who are trying to know us so that they can also help us.

The most frequently asked question people are asking is whether there is a single wing or two wings. Although this has caused some debate, many believe that we actually are a pair of wings. Each of the points that are that is adjacent to our primary personality type is a part of our wings. If you are the type nine personality the wings you have will be the type one and the type eight. Some people claim this is not the case and that everyone has a single wings. Other people claim that the wings you have do not belong to one particular type of personality. They think that since our personality has parts from each number, we are the main type , and each type is a wing of our personality. This means that there are eight wings.

A key point to remember regarding the existence of distinct wings is that certain wings are more dominant than other wings are. If you've not yet completed the Enneagram test you'll see when you receive the results, they are presented in an graph. The graph starts with your main personality being the strongest, and is followed by the other kinds of personalities , from the strongest to the weakest. The majority of the results will show all nine personality types.

Lines

One of the toughest aspects of Enneagram theory to comprehend is the lines in the theory. Although I have already discussed the lines in the past in terms of how they relate to each other, I'll be sure to give you some additional details about what the lines are.

These lines are referred to as line of influence, or the lines of motion (Cloete, n.d.). They are the method by which you can trace your character by using the Enneagram. Although we all are all of a certain type, we are able to move across the spectrum. The main type of us will stay the same, but the circumstances we encounter in our daily lives, as well as other aspects can influence our path along the lines that run through the Enneagram.

There are two kinds of lines. It is the stress line, and that of development. If you examine your most prominent personality kind on the Enneagram it will show two lines that have Arrows. One arrow will point away from your type, and is referred to as"the growth line. The other arrow is pointed towards your number type and is known as"the line of stress.

If you consider the path of growth you may think of freeing yourself from the bad personality traits. This is the line which leads us to healthier aspects of our personalities. When we follow this path, we'll be able to let our worries go and work towards self-actualization (Cloete, n.d.).

The stress line is opposite to the growth line. The line of stress focuses on the way we feel when under pressure or under stress. Most of the time, these circumstances can lead us to adopt bad habits of living. However we are able to turn the negatives to positives, which often helps to balance our lives individually (Cloete, n.d.).

Different levels of integration

The levels of integration are called the levels of integration. In each type of personality there are additional pieces that make up the persona. They are identical to your actions or motivations and attitudes. In essence, they are the pieces that create your personality. It's like the way that the pieces of the puzzle fit together to make the puzzle.

As you become aware of these levels, you'll discover that when people's moods change in their mood, for example, being more relaxed at one point but then feeling stressed the next, they're going through different phases within their personalities.

The three stages of integration are that are healthy normal, average, as well as unhealthy (Cloete, n.d.). When someone is at an unhealthy degree of integration they allow their fear or other emotions influence their behavior. When they're in a moderate stage of integration root issue is still the driving force behind their behaviour, but they can let go of certain fundamental problems. If they are at a good degree of integration they are able to let go of the most fundamental emotions as they comprehend the reason for them. This allows them to move forward and discover a better method of managing life stress and circumstances. In a way they are able to transcend the limitations they thought they were facing.

In these different levels, there are additional levels and numbers that are associated to each levels. Each level is characterized by three numbers, which correspond with how the person is performing within its degree of integration. The smaller levels are in the following order:

In the healthy range you could be at three, one, or three. One is the level of the libertarian. Level two is the psychological level as well as level 3. the social value level ("How The System Works," n.d.).

At the most basic level, you could be at levels four or five or six. Level four is the one that represents social roles or the imbalance. Level five represents the point of control over interpersonal relationships. Level six is the overcompensation level ("How The System Worked," n.d.).

In the unhealthy level you may be at level seven or eight, or even nine. Seven is the level of a violation. The eight-level is the level of compulsion or obsession. Level nine is the threshold of psychopathological destruction ("How The System works," n.d.).

The benefits of the Enneagram

People frequently use the Enneagram to find out more about their personality type for a variety of reasons. While many people are interested in their personality, other individuals want to know more in order to better understand them or someone else. Specialists in psychology and others frequently employ the Enneagram to to better understand their patients.

There are numerous benefits which are derived out of the Enneagram. The theory and test be beneficial to individuals on an individual basis but also as an entire group. In addition the Enneagram is also beneficial to those working in an organization.

Individual Level Benefits

• Help people understand why they're experiencing particular emotional or behavioral problems.

* Help people gain an understanding of their personalities so that they are able to know themselves better.

* The Enneagram helps to boost an individual's confidence and drive.

* The Enneagram can to increase compassion in other people.

* People may begin to comprehend their previous behavior patterns.
* The Enneagram helps people develop generally as they begin to comprehend their personality more fully.

Group Level Benefits

* The Enneagram helps reduce conflicts within the group.
* It also helps members of the group to be aware of where the group stands, what motivates people to act with certain manners, as well as where the strengths and weaknesses of each group member are.
* The Enneagram could help in improving the efficiency of business processes.

It improves the communication between team members, that will improve other areas of the team.

Organizational Benefits at the Level of Organization

* The Enneagram helps to regulate the political climate of an organization.
* It will enhance the leadership of an organization in general.

* The Enneagram can assist the company to overcome the fears and emotions that are associated with change.

The Enneagram is more than a simple diagram of numbers, lines and Arrows. It also does more than just reveal a person's character. You can see the above benefits it is also possible that the Enneagram helps people grow in a variety of aspects of their personal and professional lives. In addition the Enneagram will continue to assist you through the various stages of life.

Chapter 15: Enneagram Type 1: The Perfectionist

The Perfectionist often referred to as the Reformer seeks to improve things. There is always something that could be improved upon and there is never adequate enough. They have a romantic view of the world because they constantly strive to make their world better They are caught chasing for an impossible goal. They are looking to create sense in a world which is chaotic in its core This could be a problem.

If you've scored high on this test, known as Type 1 Perfectionist, you are likely to be awed by particulars and making sure everything is perfect. You're likely to be self-controlled and will put off gratification when needed, to ensure that the final outcome you want is achieved. But, you can also encounter the issue of becoming rigid and judgmental , or becoming caught up in self-righteousness and no chance of getting out.

A brief overview of the Perfectionist:

Before we dive into an deep review of the Perfectionist we should begin by going through the basics of informationBelow, you'll see a list of most basic facts you could learn regarding the Type 1 personality. The information can be broken into various categories that give you a glimpse into the thoughts of the Perfectionist.

The perfectionist is the characteristic role.

Ego fixation: Resentment

Holy idea The perfect idea

Fundamental fear: corruption or imbalance

The most fundamental desire is integrity and balance

The temptation: Hypocritical or hypercritical

Vice: Anger

Virtue: Serenity

Disintegration direction Type 4 The Romantic

Direction of Integration Type 7 The Epicure

The Type 1 person can be identified by a variety of distinct features. These traits define people of the Type 1 individual the Perfectionist and include:

Often quite straightforward during interactions

Focused on practicality, or thrifty

Devote and hardworking

Innately is a top-quality company.

Very rigid when planning plans

Focuses well

The ability to teach is innate.

An Snapshot of the Perfectionist

In person, the perfectionist is accountable. This is the person you find following the rules and making sure that everything goes as planned. They're sensible and logical. However cold they might appear when they work tirelessly, they are committed to improving the lives of all. They are determined to make a difference for the world, putting in their best and utilizing their skills to find the best method to make this improvements. They operate behind the scenes, working quietly and with a tenacious determination to control themselves and will go to the extreme to ensure they are always faithful to their commitments to the highest level of their ability.

The Idealist's Values

The most important thing is that the Perfectionist sets the standards they set for themselves. They are naturally motivated and strive to be better as they strive to make their world better. The values and beliefs they hold are enough to propel forward, without external motivations, and they seek to be accountable and do their duty. They want to ensure all employees are accountable, and they respect the integrity of others. Their character is formed by their respect for justice, loyalty and integrity.

Recognizing the Perfectionist

If you're trying to identify the Perfectionist you are searching for an organisation. Since the Perfectionist seeks perfection Their lives are typically pretty well-ordered. They tend to be straight-minded and honest. They are obligated to supply their friends with the truth , and work to make sure their goals are fulfilled.

Due to their sense of justice and enthusiasm for rules and order The Perfectionist is usually employed in areas which require a lot of self-control and commitment. They are often employed working in military settings, and thrive with a sense of order and the structure. They are also found in law enforcement with their enthusiasm for justice. They are also found in finance due to their concentration on the smallest of details. They are also in academia , with their determination to make a difference in society. Whatever you do, you'll are there is one thing that is certain that the Perfectionist is going to do all in their power to do at the highest level they can. They will ensure they're meeting and exceeding expectations at all times and adhere to the rules to the highest level, often making them the most efficient employees in their company.

Health and Fitness, The Perfectionist and Health

Naturally, the health of people is constantly changing. It can range from being healthy to unhealthy to average, and at all instances, you'll witness different aspects that make up the Perfectionist.

The Healthiest Perfectionist

If they are healthy when they are healthy, the Perfectionist is able to utilize his or her talents to the fullest extent. They can see the fact that their environment is constantly evolving and chaotic and can harness their intense desire to change and reshaping the world around their own to help bring order to this chaos. They are able to utilize their perception of justice as well as know what is fair to bring humanity towards its fullest potential. They have the ability to apply their talents and self-control determine the perfect life balance between work and family, ensuring that they find time to rest when they need to between their efforts to improve the world around them.

The Average Perfectionist

If they aren't at their most optimal, yet far from being the worst The Perfectionist can organize their life without difficulty. They have the ability to manage their lives by separating their emotions, needs and desire to make improvements. They are still as committed to improving the world around them The average Perfectionists continue to live lives in accordance with their ideals. They tend to be involved in social activities and causes that reflect the ideals they hold. They're usually very professional, putting all of their existence into their work, to the point of suppressing their emotions and needs in order to complete their tasks.

The unhealthy perfectionist

When they get unwell, Perfectionists tend to start to lose sight of reality. They might become hyper-focused on issues that aren't relevant to their argument or cause. However, this could rapidly turn into an obsession to scream out every detail to find out why there are differences in order to undermine opinions that don't line to their personal beliefs. They'll do everything they can to maintain their own image of self-worth and ensure that they can't be in error, even if they are. If they're confronted and feel they have been questioned and they are unable to resist an outburst of anger to defend themselves.

The strengths of the perfectionist

The strengths and weak points of the types of Enneagram can be divided in five categories distinct from each other: physical mental, emotional social and spiritual.

Physical Ability to recognize moderation and adhere to it, while balancing the need to be perfect with their ability to unwind and take part in self-care

Emotional: They may be able to break away from their desires for what things should be , and accept the situation as they are in the moment, while acknowledging that they are not always in control of the final results

Mental The ability to adhere to their ideals, and use their moral standards to stay in the right direction and dedicated to acting in the best way, regardless of how difficult.

Relational: They have the ability to motivate others, driving them and energizing them towards reaching their goals.

Spiritual They can remain present and not lose contact with their beliefs

The Perfectionist's weaknesses

Physical: Perfectionists usually have extreme behavior, such as eating too little or over - or under-sleep. They are at risk of developing alcohol dependence

Emotional: They are prone to an inclination to be involved in the frustration and frustration over their ideals not being realized fast enough. They may also be susceptible to OCD or depression

Mental: They are involved in thoughts of black and white and fail to recognize the hues of gray that could influence the events in the world around them

Relational: They are irritated by chaos and do not like making concessions, but they are also tending to self-righteous and judgemental behavior when they are too critical

Spiritual In the event that they fall out of connection with their ideals, they can feel deficient and corrupt, leading them to criticize themselves harshly

The Perfectionist in the course of a relationship

In an intimate relationship one can tell that the Perfectionist is very detail-oriented. They appreciate small gestures, or when their partner is punctual. If you are in a relationship with someone who is a Perfectionist You must remember to be courteous and seek permission instead of assuming that you are able to get it. The Perfectionist would like to be noticed and appreciated by a genuine person and wants someone who is as committed to their own personal growth.

In this type of relationship, it's essential to recognize the fact that you're wrong when you recognize that you're. This is only true if you're, in fact incorrect. If you do this you can remove the fog and the tendency of the Perfectionist for integrity and justice ensures that you will not be considered a slap in the face.

It is essential to understand that Perfectionists are mostly workaholics. They have a constant focus on making themselves better and others around them, and can be found working for hours. Also, you must try to stay clear of any struggle for power. It is feasible that you both are in the right direction, for yourself and both methods could be compatible.

Chapter 16: Tips for Each Type of Personality

This new understanding of personality is nothing more than a game in which you are able to evaluate yourself in comparison to others. But those who make the mistake of interpreting the Enneagram as a mere form of entertainment is missing out on an opportunity to gain valuable insight to make sense of their own life and the world surrounding them. If used correctly, the information that are provided by the Enneagram will allow you to get to the heart of who the person you're. discover and enhance your weaknesses, discover and develop your strengths, and build the skills to understand and connect to others around you."

The first time you step into the Enneagram could be both relaxing as well as jarring. On the one side, you have an entire community of people who have the same most fundamental fears and motivations, and to whom you likely connect more than you thought. However there's a vast universe of different "types" that exist that have different degrees of functioning and on what appears to be an entirely different system of values. Be cautious, however do not confuse "type" as the nature of the "true persona." It is important to recognize that the Enneagram is not static and prescriptive and static, is more descriptive that covers a spectrum of stress and integration points. Surprisingly, the parts of Enneagram type initially indicate may not be your real self, but rather the motives and fears that guide your behavior and actions. In many cases those fears and motives can create barriers that keep us from connecting to our authentic selves.

An understanding of the obstacles can become the very first stage to breaking down those barriers and revealing the depth to that you truly understand your own. After the breakdown is over, you are left with the option of offering yourself forgiveness and compassion or begin to rebuild those walls you've always known to be that separate your "personality" as well as yourself "true persona."

In recognizing the factors that are preventing us from realisation of who we are We can begin to recognize the areas of weakness as well as our flaws. Although this may not be fun for anyone, it's beneficial. It's not just that; it's crucial for anyone who wants to attain real self-knowledge and integration. The Enneagram provides a clear understanding of the different ways we cope under stress. This is the same mechanisms that helped us survive our childhood , and which we've become proficient in employing.

Through coping mechanisms like "reaction form" (One) or "overindulgence" (Eight) as well, we minimize the negative results of these defenses labeling them as valuable principles such as "virtue" or "courage." When we are in real Integration, One reveals genuine virtue, and the Eight shows real bravery, however, by relying too much on our defense mechanisms, we are at risk of being a victim of what these concepts symbolize.

The root of our anxieties and coping strategies, as well as motivations, we begin to identify the patterns that influence our decision-making process. Understanding the source of our "blind places" and the cause cause of these weaknesses have a dual impact: It equips us with the information needed to comprehend how we can overcome our shortcomings and equips us with the skills needed to maximize our strengths to ensure that we are able to be able to challenge the perceived weaknesses of our personalities.

When we are in the process of integrating, or before beginning any sort of journey toward integration, we must be aware of our own safety. In situations in which the stakes are very high We can leverage the understanding of our personal weaknesses and apply that knowledge to prevent the risk of failure, while also maximizing our chances of success.

Of of course, living a life of repression and isolation isn't exactly the way to integration and growth, however, we must look back before we begin ascending, evaluate our current situation to prepare ourselves and accept the possibility of acknowledging our flaws prior to embarking on the upward path of connecting with our real self. Once we've identified the hurts and insecurities that contribute the flaws we have, it's time to begin to work towards self-forgiveness, self-compassion and self-love. from that emerge the tools we'll need to gain a deeper understanding of ourselves.

If a Five is beginning his journey to becoming aware of himself He may want to make sure he is careful when creating an agenda for the week, deciding not to fill his schedule with activities that don't bring value to his life , so that he can maintain a good level of energy and remain present for the things that are of value to him. It is also advisable to set aside some time to be alone in activities that really refresh his mind, be it reading, watching lectures or taking part in a particular interest. Through recognizing his limitations and advancing to a place where he's able to flourish inside them, the person could eventually be able to direct his attention on other areas and try to exceed those limits just a little.

Instead of denigrating our weaknesses, or looking to "correct" them through countering their effects and pushing ourselves to the limit Instead of denying our weaknesses or pushing them to the limit, the Enneagram assists us to identify the root of our weaknesses . It also helps us create a sense self-compassion, from which we can grow and progress toward integration.

Simply said, there's bound to be things that you're skilled at, but there are also certain things that will can make you appear like an untrained fish trying to climb the tree. It's healthy and good to push your self from time to time but you must avoid the psychological traps that result from constantly self-identifying as "the fish who can't climb the tree."

Do people gravitate towards you for advice when they need it (Two)? Do they contact you when they're looking to forget about their worries and have a good time (Seven)? Do they ask you for information, pens or Band-Aids, etc. Knowing that 9 times out of 10 you're ready for anything (Six)?

The Enneagram will to clarify those aspects that are just natural to you. And, better is to aid you in understanding why this happens. If you're referred to as"charming" (Three), then you need to consider your motivations "charmer" (Three), analyzes your motivations and then you begin to shift your focus away from that these motives are in service to you towards a place where your "charm" is actually an act of self-love where you truly recognize the positive in people. In place instead of "flattery," you offer "loving truths." Instead of "performing," you are "connecting."

The nine kinds have an inherent ability to view the world in an individual way. Each type provide a crucial and valuable contribution to humanity. Many of the Enneagram literature focuses on the flaws each types has. And it's not without a reason. What aids us in identifying the characteristics of our type is our weaknesses that prevent us from being like others, the factors that prevent our ability to feel empathy for those who are not as we do. But, once we understand our weaknesses and overcoming them, we can overcome them.

After you've learned self-compassion, it's time to shift to empathy. This, when practiced and practiced, can result in having compassion for those around you. What the Enneagram does this by ensuring that it equips us with the tools needed to look at the world through another's eyes. Although we all have a dominant type, the majority of us have at most one or two ways to connect to different kinds. Have you ever been frightened, curious or self-righteous? The fact that your predominant kind of person experiences some of these emotions more frequently than others does not mean that you don't, in some way share a commonality in common with all eight kinds. When we look at the motives and fears of the different types, we might be able to identify little to a certain extent with each of the numbers. We will begin to comprehend the possibility to feel different elements of us in an than usual way and feel overwhelmed by certain thoughts patterns that our personality tends to suppress or avoid.

When we're in touch to empathy and compassion, we are able to work towards a position of compassion towards others, in which we are not just aware of how people might be feeling, but we also decide to be a part of the solution by interacting with others. If we can understand the different ways people perceive our actions and how we translate our actions into expressions of love and value and value, we can begin to discover innovative ways to alter our attitude and how we communicate. We can begin to see how to communicate with others with a manner that communicates values and affection in the way we wish to convey it.

When you realize that a Four-year-old has an intense need to feel each emotion, but also understand it, you may decide to let him speak about the issue he's experiencing. Instead of providing an immediate solution or alternative, you could challenge yourself to be in suffering with him, as difficult as it might be, and then communicate with him by being present.

If you realize that a Nine will likely to deny her own needs in order to promote harmony, you may think to provide alternatives when you are deciding on the best way to go about it instead of asking "Do you wish to do [insert the thing you would like to accomplish[insert what you want to do]?" Along with offering options, you can consider using words that promote the idea of the nine in your lives is important and that the voice of her, her needs and ideas are important equally.

As we strive to be integrated and integration, we will hopefully come to a place where the concepts of love and value according to our understanding is not defined by superficial factors connected to our particular "type" or the way we view someone else's "type" instead, but by the knowledge that value is inherent in us , and that love surrounds us. Integration starts when we acknowledge our flaws and decide to cultivate self-compassion. As we continue to develop and turn our attention to the outside our empathy is allowed to influence our perception of the world. The journey of integration reaches the point where we are able to commit to our empathy and demonstrate compassion for others in our lives. This focus on our outer appearance brings us closer to our fellow humans and ultimately it allows us discover and connect with our inner self.

Chapter 17: Establishing Rapport for Telephone Coaching

What speed do you think that your clients who coach will be able to determine if they will benefit from a specific conversation? Psychologists have now agreed that memories are made during conversations. The impressions are repeatedly tested and every time they're correct and reinforced. If you are practicing for 30 minutes then you will have only five minutes left to establish the right tone to be successful.

What tools do you have in place to connect, improve and test with the movement of your clients? Customers who coach are expecting them to change direction or move with confidence? In the beginning you must be more than taking the first step and create an exact pattern. The process of moving throughout the sequence (connecting and strengthening, as well as shifting) suggests that you're ready to incorporate this pattern into the coaching session.

The first report is not fast to be written in words. It develops from the vocal characteristics like the tone, pitch and rhythm. The vocal features can be controlled through a wider voice desire that connects the other end of the phone to the individual. Although you won't be able to see the facial expression of the person, you'll hear subtle variations in the sound that permit automatic changes to indicate that two individuals are related. Be wary of voices that do not fit. Prepare yourself to connect and concentrate on your client before you pick up the phone.

You can demonstrate your interest and connect by listening to your client by accurately reciting the words, jargons or syntax that the customer has offered. The ability to paraphrase what you've learned will change the meaning If you've established an excellent connection with your customer, they will take the new meaning when you paraphrase. If not, the test was not successful and you'll have to fix it. It is better to stay with what you hear in the speech spoken by your customer. This will show that you are attentive.

Conclusion

What next? I believe the next step is to keep connected to the Enneagram as well as your Enneatype. Once you have a clear understanding of who you are and what your strength and weakness are you'll be well-equipped to enter any of your relationships with full knowledge and appreciation of the potential and power that is the power of the Enneagram.

I'd like to believe that, regardless of the kind of person you are, or what type you have in your family The knowledge you've gained through this book can help to strengthen relationships, improve lives, and reduce conflicts. However, there is no limit to knowledge, and the Enneagram is more extensive than an article like this could provide. If you're interested in finding out details about Enneagram it is possible to go deeper into the world of the Enneagram to discover more about yourself and those you care about.

www.ingramcontent.com/pod-product-compliance
Lightning Source LLC
Chambersburg PA
CBHW071837080526
44589CB00012B/1025